# Earl Warren

*Justice for All*

OXFORD
PORTRAITS

# Earl Warren

*Justice for All*

Christine L. Compston

OXFORD
UNIVERSITY PRESS

*For Steve*

# OXFORD
## UNIVERSITY PRESS

Oxford   New York
Athens   Auckland   Bangkok   Bogotá   Buenos Aires   Cape Town
Chennai   Dar es Salaam   Delhi   Florence   Hong Kong   Istanbul   Karachi
Kolkata   Kuala Lumpur   Madrid   Melbourne   Mexico City   Mumbai   Nairobi
Paris   São Paulo   Shanghai   Singapore   Taipei   Tokyo   Toronto   Warsaw
and associated companies in Berlin   Ibadan

Copyright © 2001 by Christine L. Compston
Published by Oxford University Press, Inc.
198 Madison Avenue, New York, New York  10016
www.oup.com

Oxford is a registered trademark of Oxford University Press

Design: Greg Wozney
Layout: Alexis Siroc
Picture research: Jennifer Smith

Library of Congress Cataloging-in-Publication Data

Compston, Christine L.
    Earl Warren : justice for all / Christine L. Compston.
        p. cm. - (Oxford portraits)
    Includes bibliographical references and index.
    Summary: Examines the life of the influential Supreme Court justice who made
decisions that were politically unpopular during such notable twentieth-century events
as World War II and the civil rights movement.
      ISBN-13: 978-0-19-513001-0
      ISBN 0-19-513001-4
        1. Warren, Earl, 1891-1974--Juvenile literature. 2. Judges--United
States--Biography--Juvenile literature. 3. United States. Supreme
Court—Biography—Juvenile literature. [1. Warren, Earl, 1891-1974. 2. Judges. 3. United
States. Supreme Court--Biography.] I. Title. II. Series.

KF8745.W3 C66 2001
347.73'2634--dc21
[B]                                                                   2001036904

9 8 7 6 5 4 3 2

Printed in the United States of America
on acid-free paper

*On the cover:* Governor Earl Warren in 1948.
*Frontispiece:* Warren on the steps of the Supreme Court on his first day as chief
justice of the United States, October 5, 1953.

# CONTENTS

# INTRODUCTION

Earl Warren's opinion in the case of *Brown* v. *Board of Education of Topeka, Kansas,* his first major decision as chief justice of the United States, is considered by many to be the most important Supreme Court decision of the 20th century. The ruling ended segregation in public schools and marked a turning point in the civil rights movement.

Warren himself believed that the Court's decisions requiring states to reapportion, or adjust the boundaries of their legislative districts in order to give each voter an equal voice in the electoral process, were of greater significance. If the principle of "one man, one vote" had been in existence 50 years earlier, he argued, "we would have saved ourselves acute racial troubles. Many of our problems would have been solved a long time ago if everyone had this right to vote and his vote counted the same as everybody else's. Most of these problems could have been solved through the political process rather than through the courts."

As Warren's remarks reveal, one of his goals was to make the American political system more responsive to the needs of its citizens. The reapportionment decisions made during his tenure as chief justice were the culmination of a career committed to the ideals of democratic government.

As an elected official—serving as district attorney of Alameda County, California, then as attorney general and governor of his home state—Warren instituted reforms to improve management, free government from the influence of special interests, and eliminate corruption. Nominally a Republican, he tended to favor Democratic programs and frequently found himself supporting Democratic candidates. When running for political office, he often presented himself as a candidate committed to the general welfare rather than to a specific party's agenda.

Warren's record, however, was not untarnished. During his term as attorney general of California, which coincided with the entrance of the United States into World War II, he was an outspoken advocate for the internment, or confinement, of Japanese Americans, a position that he soon came to regret. Although he never publicly apologized for his role in this decision, his later actions showed that he learned a great deal from his mistake. As governor, he imposed guidelines for the resettlement of the Japanese Americans, protecting them from additional hardships. As chief justice, he led the Court in the battle to end segregation and other forms of discrimination despite tremendous hostility directed toward him personally.

Over time, Warren enlarged his notion of democracy to include equality of opportunity and "equal justice under law." While serving in elective office, his attempts to achieve those goals by challenging discrimination based on race or gender met with only limited success. Warren used the independence of the judiciary—the fact that justices are appointed for life, as opposed to politicians who are elected for designated terms and must keep people happy in order to be re-elected—to lead the Court in making decisions that were extremely unpopular with large segments of the American population but consistent with his own sense of justice. During his time on the Court, he applied the principles of fairness and equality to a wide range of cases involving civil rights, freedom of expression, political participation, and criminal rights.

Because a number of Warren's most important opinions were based on moral and ethical concerns rather than legal and constitutional issues, he was frequently criticized for expanding the role of the judiciary and exercising powers not granted by the Constitution or established practice. He was, however, respected and even admired by people who shared his belief that judges should intervene when the political system fails and the nation's laws discriminate.

*Eleven-year-old Earl keeps a firm hold on his dog Spot. Earl loved animals, and as a child spent much of his time with his pets—house dogs, hunting dogs, a sheep, an eagle, pet chickens, rabbits, and a burro named Jack.*

# 1

# GOLDEN
# OPPORTUNITIES

Earl Warren's parents were Scandinavians who had emigrated to the United States as young children. His mother, Crystal Hernlund, came from Sweden, his father, Methias (known as Matt) Varran from Norway. Earl's uncle changed the family's name to Warren after they settled in the United States.

Though they were eager to take advantage of the opportunities available in their new land, both families also preserved certain traits associated with their Scandinavian heritage. Among these was a reluctance to show one's feelings, as well as a tendency to protect one's private life from public scrutiny. This reserve, which Warren maintained throughout his entire career as a public servant, helps explain why we have few first-hand accounts of his private life and why those records say so little that is of a personal nature. Warren's *Memoirs,* which he wrote after he retired, deal almost exclusively with his public service.

The families of both his parents settled in the Midwest. The Hernlunds moved to Minneapolis after the Great Fire of 1871 destroyed their home in Chicago. The Warrens, in contrast, chose to farm. The family struggled to make a living, first in Illinois and later in Iowa. Meeting with little success, the parents were forced to arrange for the two sons, Matt and his older brother Ole, to earn their room, board, and school tuition by working on a neighboring farm.

When Matt completed the seventh grade, the two brothers went to Chicago in search of better opportunities. They were able to support themselves for a few years before Ole contracted tuberculosis and died. For the rest of his life, Matt blamed his brother's death on their poverty. This experience shaped his values, convincing him of the need to live frugally in order always to have money on hand to meet family emergencies.

Alone, Matt moved to Minneapolis in 1885, where he met and married Crystal Hernlund. Their first child, Ethel, was born a year later. Like many other midwesterners, the Warrens were attracted to California by its climate as well as the job opportunities there. They moved first to San Diego, in 1889, but had settled in Los Angeles, in a small house near the railroad depot, by the time their son Earl was born on March 19, 1891.

Matt Warren was a car repairman and inspector for the Southern Pacific Railroad. Organized in 1865, the Southern Pacific quickly established a monopoly on train service in California. In many respects, the railroad contributed to the growth and prosperity of the state. It employed more workers and owned more land than any other company in the state, and it provided transportation essential to most other businesses statewide, hauling raw materials as well as finished products to prospective buyers.

Exercising its power, the Southern Pacific invested heavily in state politics. The owners successfully "persuaded"— paid—members of the Railroad Commission not to lower the rates railroads could charge for their services. Not until the Santa Fe Railroad opened a parallel line from Oakland to Bakersfield in 1896 did freight rates start to drop. In the meantime, the Southern Pacific raked in huge profits. Railroad employees, including Matt Warren, experienced the tremendous power of the Southern Pacific firsthand when they decided to join a nationwide strike called by the American Railway Union in 1894.

The strike had its roots in a community just south of Chicago that was owned and operated by the Pullman Palace Car Company. The Pullman Company, which made dining cars, parlor cars, and sleeper cars, had responded to the economic depression of 1893 by sharply reducing wages. All Pullman workers lived in company-owned housing, bought groceries at company-owned stores, and kept their money in company-owned banks. When Pullman decided to reduce wages, it did not reduce its rents or the prices it charged. As a result, the cost of living exceeded what workers were being paid.

The workers protested, but the owners refused to bargain. Faced with no alternative, about 2,500 Pullman employees called a strike on May 11 and urged other railroad workers to show their sympathy by joining the walkout. The American Railway Union agreed to participate, and by the end of June more than 20,000 of its members in Chicago and an additional 40,000 in other parts of the country were walking the picket lines. Matt Warren was one of them.

The strike, which lasted for three months, resulted in defeat for the union when federal troops were brought in to break the impasse. Matt Warren had earned only $70 a month before the strike. When it ended, he lost his job and was blacklisted until the Southern Pacific opened repair shops just outside Bakersfield. Because the company was desperate for skilled workers, they removed Matt from the blacklist and offered him a job. The Warrens moved to Bakersfield in 1896.

Bakersfield was a boomtown during Earl Warren's childhood. It was dominated by the railroad until the turn of the century, when oil was discovered nearby. Both industries offered opportunities for men to make a lot of money in a short time. Along with families like the Warrens, the

population consisted of "boomers," men who moved from town to town, living in hotels and boardinghouses, taking whatever jobs came their way and spending their earnings at the local gambling joints and saloons; Basque shepherds, from the hills of northern Spain, who tended herds

*Earl was three years old when the family—Crystal, Earl, Methias, and Ethel—posed for this formal portrait. The Warrens were still living in Los Angeles, but they would soon move as a result of his father's involvement in the Pullman strike.*

in the hills outside town; and Chinese immigrants, brought to California to lay track for the railroads, who were subjected to racist and discriminatory treatment.

Earl's own parents set a very different example from that offered by the boomers. The Warrens lived simply. By his own example, Matt Warren instilled in his children the value of education, hard work, and saving for future needs. Looking back on his childhood, Earl observed of his father that he "lived a Spartan life, which meant a more or less Spartan life for both [of his parents].... [H]e adopted those habits so that he would be sure that my sister and I would have a good education."

Earl entered school a year early because he already knew how to read and write. He skipped the second grade, but, despite his father's insistence on the importance of education, failed to distinguish himself as a scholar. He did well in subjects he liked: history, English, and French. As he later explained, Kern County Union High School was "not a particularly inspirational atmosphere."

Encouraged by his parents, Earl learned to play the clarinet. He was a talented musician, and by the time he was in high school he was a member of the local musicians' union—a charter member of Bakersfield Local 263 of the

American Federation of Musicians—and playing with local dance bands. This experience provided a good source of income for him as a young adult and also taught him respect for labor unions. He carried a union card for the rest of his life. When he campaigned for the office of state attorney general in 1938, the musicians' union endorsed him.

While still a teenager, Warren decided to become a lawyer. In his memoirs, he admitted that he did not know exactly what motivated that decision. "On my way to and from high school," he wrote, "I rode my bicycle through the courthouse square. Often on my way home I would stop to watch some trial just to see some of the lawyers in action. I can only guess that I admired their ability to stand on their feet and speak with ease before a court and jury, an ability I did not have even in the schoolroom with my classmates."

Along with seeing local lawyers in action, small town Americans entertained their intellects with what were called Chautauqua lecturers. The Chautauqua Assembly was founded

*Chester Avenue and 19th Street formed the main intersection of Bakersfield around 1904. The electric power lines, streetcars, and automobile serve as reminders of the dramatic changes that were transforming life in America's cities.*

in 1874 to further the education of teachers. Initially, the summer programs held on the shores of Chautauqua Lake in western New York state focused on religious studies, but the curriculum quickly expanded to include literature, history, sociology, and science. By the late 19th century, "Chautauquas" had become traveling shows offering lectures, concerts, and performances of various sorts.

Matt Warren regularly attended the local Chautauqua and occasionally took his son with him. "Of all the lectures that I heard in my youth," Earl later wrote, a talk given by Dr. Russell H. Conwell, a Baptist minister and founder of Temple University in Philadelphia, entitled "Acres of Diamonds" made the "greatest impression." The theme of the lecture, that one need not search the world to find opportunity and riches, was illustrated by the story of a Persian who sold his property and went in search of great wealth. After the Persian died, the person who had bought his land found the most valuable diamond in the world in his backyard.

From the time he was nine years old, Earl held a job every summer. One of his assignments was as a "swamper," or helper, for the local iceman. Working seven days a week, eight to nine hours a day, he carried blocks of ice into customers' homes. He received 25 cents a day and a 10-to-15-pound block of ice for his own family. When he was 12, he drove the delivery wagon for the local baker, earning 25 cents a day and cookies to take home. He also delivered newspapers—the *Los Angeles Herald* and the *Bakersfield Californian*—before and after school.

Earl was employed in various jobs by the Southern Pacific from the time he was 15 until he graduated from law school. His first job there was as a callboy. During the summer months, he worked 12 hours a day, 6 days a week, for 22 cents an hour, rounding up the crews scheduled for the day's runs. Over time, he held positions in the car shops, machine shops, and baggage rooms. These jobs, he noted, were "meaningful because I was dealing with people as they

worked for a gigantic corporation that dominated the economic and political life of the community. I saw that power
exercised and the hardship that followed in its wake."

As an employee of the Southern Pacific, he concluded
that workers who earned little for their labor tended to
waste their money on frivolous entertainment. He saw families subjected to poverty as a result of gambling and other
forms of vice, many of which were allowed or even encouraged by local and state governments.

Earl entered the University of California at Berkeley in
the fall of 1908. Established in 1868, the university had
acquired a reputation in the late 19th century for powerless
presidents and disorderly students. By the time Earl arrived
on campus, however, Benjamin Ide Wheeler, appointed president in 1899, had established himself as a forceful, effective
administrator. Unlike most university presidents at that
time, he treated students as adults. He allowed them to
establish their own government, propose regulations, and
investigate student disciplinary cases.

Under Wheeler's leadership, the university was earning
a reputation as an academic institution of national stature.
By 1908, it had a total student enrollment of 3,100 and a
faculty of 300, many of them distinguished scholars. Earl,
however, still was not a serious student. "I was more concerned with adequacy than profundity," he later wrote. "I
was more interested in the university as a community of
lively, stimulating people than as a community of scholars. I
had no intention of failing, but neither did I have a burning
desire for knowledge which my parents' sacrifices for my
education should have called for."

This was the first time Earl had been away from home
and family, and he found it a "wonderful new world—large,
dynamic, enthusiastic, friendly, and with unlimited freedom." He was invited to join the La Junta Club, a residen-
tial club located near the south entrance to the campus. He
joined a variety of other clubs, served on committees for

university social events, and played clarinet in the university's band. He also played bridge, read poetry, and participated in sports. And he made lifelong friends.

Earl Warren's friendship with Walter Arthur Gordon, for example, originated at Berkeley. Gordon, the son of a janitor and the grandson of a slave, ranked as one of the university's outstanding athletes and was named an All-American football player. He and Warren spent many afternoons boxing in the college gymnasium. After graduation, their career paths crossed frequently. Gordon served for 14 years as head of the Alameda County branch of the National Association for the Advancement of Colored People (NAACP). In 1945, in his capacity as governor, Warren appointed him chairman of the adult branch of the California prison system, and in 1955, early in his career as chief justice, he swore in his friend as governor of the Virgin Islands. Three years after that, Gordon became a federal district judge.

Warren's undergraduate years coincided with the emergence of the Progressive Party as a dominant force in American politics. Thomas Harrison Reed, a faculty member in Berkeley's political science department who was an outspoken, enthusiastic Progressive, sparked Warren's interest in reform politics. Warren attended rallies for Progressive and Socialist candidates in San Francisco and Berkeley and served as a poll-watcher in San Francisco's Mission District in the 1910 election. Two years later, he made his way to Sacramento to hear Wisconsin's Senator Robert La Follette campaign for the Republican nomination for President.

Taking advantage of an accelerated program, Warren entered law school during his final year of college. Berkeley's law school, Boalt Hall, had just opened and employed a faculty of 5 to teach the 79 students. He took prescribed courses—contracts, property, torts (civil cases involving injury or damage), and criminal law—but objected to the case-study method of teaching that had been imported from Harvard Law School. Warren wanted a straightforward, practical introduction to the study of law, but what the case method provided was a theoretical understanding of legal principles drawn from a chronological study of important cases. He refused to speak in class and, despite the fact that the law school forbade students to work in law offices, took a job with a local firm in order to acquire a working knowledge of his field. Fifteen men and one woman graduated in his class and were all admitted to the California bar without having to take an examination. At that time, a vote of the faculty was sufficient for graduates of the University of California, Hastings College of Law in San Francisco, and the University of Southern California to be allowed to practice in the state.

Warren hoped to become a trial lawyer, but his first two jobs out of law school were essentially clerical positions. He began his career in the law department of the Associated Oil Company in San Francisco, where he was expected to run errands for the senior staff and was given little or no credit for his professional contributions. At the end of a year, he accepted a position with a law firm in Oakland, Robinson and Robinson, which offered a more pleasant work atmosphere but not much more challenge. There he checked contracts, read leases, maintained legal records, did research for senior partners, and occasionally prepared briefs. His only so-called courtroom experience consisted of serving as office messenger, delivering legal documents to the local courthouse. This was not the sort of career he had envisioned for himself.

Based on his experiences at Berkeley, Warren realized the importance of developing a professional network. Because the local bar association no longer held meetings, Warren and other recent graduates formed the Young Lawyers' Club of Alameda County. He was elected president. In contrast to a formal bar association, the club did not focus on professional issues but served rather as a social organization, holding meetings every other week to which speakers were invited, and providing a forum in which young lawyers could establish contacts. Eventually, the members persuaded the local bar association to resume its meetings and elect new officers. Just three years out of law school, Warren was elected vice-president of the third largest bar association in the state.

*During World War I, Camp Lewis was the training ground for the 91st Division. Warren recalled that when the first group of recruits arrived at the camp, "we lived almost in squalor for weeks until some new issues arrived. We were immediately started on close order drill and long marches around American Lake four miles away, and through the forests which surrounded it."*

Dissatisfied with the level of responsibility he had been given at the Robinson firm, Warren made plans with two law school classmates, Chris Fox and Thomas Ledwich, to establish their own practice. They made arrangements with Peter J. Crosby, an experienced trial lawyer, to form a partnership; Crosby was to receive a majority of the earnings and the three young lawyers were to do a majority of the work.

Before they could go forward with their plans, World War I began. Soon after the United States entered the war on April 6, 1917, Warren applied for admission to the First Officers Training Camp, but was not accepted. His second attempt also failed—this time for health reasons—so he enlisted in the army as an infantry private and began his

A LINE-UP FOR OUT-GOING BUSSES.   CAMP LEWIS, WASH.

military career at what is now Fort Lewis, Washington. At the end of four weeks, he was promoted to first sergeant in a unit of 250 men.

The camp had opened the day before the new recruits from Oakland arrived. As Warren recalled, training itself was limited by a lack of resources: "For guns to drill with, we had wooden objects fashioned after the general outlines of a gun." After serving for four months in Camp Lewis, Warren was admitted to the officers' training program at Camp Lee in Petersburg, Virginia, where he specialized in bayonet combat. During his time in the South, he joined his fellow officers in exploring Civil War battle sites. "We also went to Richmond," he later wrote. "Our first visit there was on Memorial Day, and I remember how shocked we from Camp Lewis were because the city was bedecked in Confederate flags. They were everywhere, and not an American flag was to be seen."

Warren was not shipped overseas. Instead, he was promoted to first lieutenant and assigned to Camp MacArthur in Waco, Texas, as an instructor at the Central Infantry Officers' Training School. Before he had a chance to assume his new duties, the war ended, on November 11, 1918.

*Ezra DeCoto, right, congratulates Warren on his appointment as district attorney for Alameda County. Warren described his former boss as "honest and kindly," but "not particularly aggressive." When DeCoto decided to accept an appointment as State Railroad Commissioner, he supported Warren's promotion to county district attorney.*

CHAPTER

2

# THE NATION'S BEST DISTRICT ATTORNEY

In the early 20th century, Progressives dominated politics in California. Big business and party politicians had gained control over local and state governments, using their influence to secure privileges and increase profits at the expense of ordinary citizens. Progressive reformers—primarily members of the white middle class who were active in both the Republican and Democratic parties—were determined to restore control to the people, by whom they meant individuals like themselves. Reformers with this goal in mind developed proposals that were intended to end corruption, reduce the power of party leaders, and empower voters.

Hiram W. Johnson, a lawyer and native Californian, emerged as the leader of the California Progressives by 1908 as a result of his role in the corruption investigation launched against the government of San Francisco. The principal target of the investigation, Mayor Abraham Ruef, was charged with accepting bribes in return for political favors. When Francis J. Heney, the prosecutor, was shot in the courtroom, his assistant, Johnson, took over the case and won a conviction against Ruef. Two years later, in 1910, Johnson was elected governor of California.

As governor, Hiram Johnson introduced a variety of reforms aimed at limiting the political influence of the Southern Pacific Railroad and strengthening democratic government. He inaugurated the use of initiatives and referendums, procedures that allow voters to propose and pass laws through the ballot. He also urged adoption of the direct primary election, which enables voters rather than party conventions to choose candidates, and of a system for cross-filing, which permits candidates to run in the other party's primary as well as their own.

The Progressives' legislative program also included specific protections for workers: financial compensation for individuals injured on the job, regulation of child labor, limits on the number of hours women could work, establishment of a minimum wage, and provisions for factory inspections to ensure safe working conditions. At Johnson's urging, the legislature empowered California's Railroad Commission to determine what the railroads could charge for their services and provided for the regulation of public utilities, including gas, water, electricity, the telephone, and the telegraph.

Earl Warren was attracted to this reform movement not only by its practical aspects but also because of its emphasis on honest government. When he returned to California at the end of World War I, he pursued his interest in politics and accepted a position as clerk of the Judiciary Committee for the State Assembly. The legislative session, he later wrote, was "*not* inspirational" but definitely "informative." He learned a great deal about how the legislature operated, the roles played by elected representatives, and the lobbying system, "in both its enlightening and its more sinister forms." As he later observed, "I learned more things to avoid than to follow."

*Hiram Johnson, who promised to fight for the people against corrupt party politics and big business, helped found the Progressive Party in 1912. He served as governor of California from 1911 to 1917 and as United States senator from 1917 to 1935.*

When the legislative session ended in early summer, Warren moved on. For a short time he shared a law office in Oakland, then accepted a job as deputy city attorney. At the end of World War I, Oakland had a population just under 200,000. Most of these residents were white, Protestant, and Republican; many were newcomers who had migrated to California with high hopes and little money. As deputy attorney, Warren earned just $200 a month, a sum comparable to slightly more than $1,900 per month in current terms, but he gained useful experience. In this position he advised the city's officers and board members on the interpretation of city laws, wrote briefs, and represented the city of Oakland in a wide range of lawsuits.

On May 1, 1920, Warren began working for the district attorney for Alameda County, Ezra DeCoto. He took a temporary cut in salary, to $150 a month, to gain courtroom experience. Unlike the other deputies, who engaged in private practice to supplement their low earnings, Warren regularly worked long hours—six days a week and most evenings—on both criminal and civil cases. He learned about all the aspects of county government and quickly earned a reputation, as a result of his hard work and good instincts, for knowing what was going on. In 1925, when DeCoto resigned his position to accept an appointment to the state Railroad Commission, the Board of Supervisors appointed Warren to complete his term.

Warren's salary had risen to $5,000 a year by 1925; as district attorney he earned $7,000. This increase made it possible for him to marry Nina Palmquist Meyers, a Swedish immigrant he had met in April 1921 at a Sunday afternoon swimming party. The Palmquists, like Warren's parents, had first settled in the Midwest before moving to California. Nina's mother died when she was a small child. Her father, a Baptist minister and an osteopathic doctor, remarried. He died when Nina was 13 years old, leaving the family with limited resources. Nina and her two sisters

had to leave school to work. When she was 20, Nina married a promising young musician named Grover Meyers, but he died only a year later, just three weeks after their son James was born. Nina then moved in with her stepmother, who took care of Jimmy while Nina worked, first as a salesperson, then as the manager of a women's dress shop.

According to their children, Earl and Nina adored each other. Warren confessed in his memoirs that he was "immediately attracted to her." Although "she was as busy as I was," he wrote, "we found time to become acquainted and often went to dinner and the theater on Saturday evenings. We also spent a part of our Sundays together whenever possible. It wasn't long until we were thinking in terms of marriage, but we decided to wait until my income was sufficient to properly maintain a home." Aware of societal changes that had taken place during his lifetime, Warren explained that "social patterns were different then, and I would have felt humiliated if my wife had been compelled to work." The couple dated for two years before becoming engaged, then waited another two years to be married.

The wedding, a small family affair, took place at the First Baptist Church in Oakland on October 14, 1925. When Warren arrived at the church, he found two of his colleagues parked across the street, so he invited them in to attend the ceremony. These two friends had secretly arranged for cars from the highway patrol to assemble nearby. When the wedding was over and the newlyweds set off to honeymoon in Victoria, British Columbia, the patrol cars—sirens blaring—led the way as far as the county line.

Earl Warren's commitment to honesty and independence was evident in the 1926 election, when he had to campaign for a four-year term to keep his job. With the exception of $150 contributions from each of his three top assistants, he refused all campaign donations. Instead, he used his own money to pay for expenses, which he kept to a minimum. In the days before radio and television, political campaigns depended heavily on personal contact with the voters and on receiving local newspaper coverage. Warren used opportunities to speak at club meetings, luncheons, and special events to obtain free press coverage. This strategy worked; he carried all but two precincts.

Warren liked being a manager. He had the ability to organize and oversee office operations, and he understood the benefits that resulted from efficient administration. As district attorney, he had a staff of 25 lawyers, 10 inspectors, and a personal secretary, in addition to a large group of clerical workers. Because salaries were low, he usually hired recent law school graduates and World War I veterans who were willing to work hard in order to gain good experience. He expected his staff to have the highest moral and ethical standards, to be free of strong party affiliations, and to devote themselves to their work.

Warren's emphasis on effective administration along with his strong commitment to public service shaped his office policies and procedures. For example, the law required that cases be tried within 60 days of arraignment— the formal process of bringing charges against a defendant —but Warren urged speeding up the process. His goal was to avoid creating a backlog of cases, a problem that had previously been solved by allowing the accused to bargain for reduced punishments by admitting to lesser crimes. This strategy, called plea bargaining, had been used in Alameda County since the 1880s. By the beginning of the 20th century it was being employed in one-third of the felony, or major criminal, cases in the county. To correct this situation, Warren adopted a policy of bringing cases to trial within 30 days of charges being filed. For years, he claimed, his office managed to try even the most important cases within this shorter period.

Warren quickly demonstrated his intention to eliminate corruption in local government. One of his first targets was Burton F. Becker, a leader of the local Ku Klux Klan, who had been elected sheriff of Alameda County in November 1926. Becker had promised in his campaign to eliminate crime. However, even before assuming his new office in January 1927, he met with bootleggers, slot-machine owners, and others involved in illegal money-making operations to make deals by which he would receive payments in return for allowing these criminal activities to continue. After learning of these arrangements, Warren called Becker in to his office in January, February, and again in March to warn the sheriff that his actions would be investigated if he did not change his ways. But Becker resented Warren's interference and only expanded his corrupt practices, forcing the district attorney to take action. Warren convinced his Board of Supervisors to fund a $30,000 investigation of Becker. In 1930, the sheriff was tried and convicted of collecting bribes from illegal vice operations in Oakland and Emeryville.

*Warren, left, consults with Fred Smith, the principal witness for the prosecution in a graft trial held in 1930. Warren aggressively challenged corrupt practices in local government while serving as district attorney for Alameda County.*

Warren launched another major investigation against Becker's deputy sheriff, William Parker. Warren's office had found evidence of graft in street-paving contracts and traced the corruption to Parker, whom Sheriff Becker had appointed Road Commissioner. In an illegal arrangement that benefited both Parker and the paving company, the Greater Oakland Construction Company paid Parker one-half cent for each square foot of road it paved, and in turn the company charged the city considerably more than it required to make a fair profit.

When Warren was preparing to bring this case to trial, he learned of a book about the San Francisco corruption trials in 1908 and 1909, in which Hiram Johnson had established his reputation as the leader of the Progressives. From this source Warren learned that the delays in bringing those cases to trial and the further delays used to obstruct the proceedings once the trials were under way had resulted in a loss of public interest and only one conviction among the many who were prosecuted.

Warren decided not to allow the same thing to happen in the Parker case. In an effort to shore up public support,

*text contiues on page 29*

# LESSONS FROM HISTORY: THE SAN FRANCISCO GRAFT PROSECUTION

*Throughout his life, Warren devoted much of his discretionary time to reading: for a couple of hours in the morning before work and several hours in the evening before bed. For the most part, his reading was work related rather than recreational. In his memoirs Warren describes the importance of "The System" as Uncovered by the San Francisco Graft Prosecution, by Franklin Hichborn, to his own handling of the Deputy Sheriff William Parker graft case. Hichborn, who had already established a reputation for exposing corruption in the California state government, used the graft trial of Mayor Abraham Ruef to reveal the powerful role of the Southern Pacific machine—what he calls the "System"—in local government. In San Francisco, Hichborn wrote, "a few citizens, in spite of ridicule, abuse, social ostracism and business opposition, stood firm for civic righteousness. This made San Francisco's attack upon the 'System' possible and stirred the 'System' to extraordinary resistance." Here Warren describes how the book affected him.*

We had been working on [the Parker case] for a long time. ...I had read extensively about graft trials in other states, and how most of them had failed because it was made to appear that one political gang was merely trying to displace another. One book in particular made a deep impression on me.... The book was entitled *The System*. I...read it, not once, but a number of times. No book I have ever read did me as much good in my public career as that one did. It was a carefully documented account of everything that had occurred, and told how the entire reform movement in San Francisco failed because of delays in the courts.

he released grand jury testimony to the press on a daily basis. Throughout the trial, he worked closely with the judges to prevent the use of delaying tactics. These strategies—along with vigorous examinations of the witnesses at the trial— resulted in guilty verdicts for Parker and several of his associates.

Writing about these cases after his retirement, Warren observed that the tactics his office had used would not have been acceptable at a later time. In particular, he expressed reservations about the pressures his office had placed on the managers of the paving company when they attempted to exercise their 5th Amendment right against self-incrimination. He pointed out, however, that few guidelines for prosecutors had been in place in the 1920s when these trials had taken place.

Nevertheless, the public at that time held certain assumptions regarding constitutional protections, and Warren was sharply criticized for his handling of what came to be called the *Point Lobos* murder case. On March 22, 1936, four men boarded the freighter *Point Lobos,* which was docked at the Oakland waterfront, and murdered the chief engineer, George Alberts. Their motive was apparently related to the fact that the maritime union, a tough labor organization whose membership included communists as well as those who sympathized with them, was on strike, and its leaders resented Alberts's outspoken opposition to communism.

Warren allowed his investigators to employ informants to identify suspects, to use eavesdropping devices to gather evidence, and to carry out intensive interrogations without having lawyers present, a practice that led both to confessions and to further accusations of wrongdoing. The labor union, challenging the constitutionality of these tactics, claimed that Warren used the case to undermine their bargaining power for a better contract. To publicize these accusations the union bought time on local radio stations. During the trial, more than a thousand picketers marched outside the courthouse in protest. In the end, however, the jury found all four men guilty of second-degree murder, unplanned but intentional killing.

The defense attorneys immediately sought to disqualify the presiding judge, Frank M. Ogden. He had been one of Warren's assistants before being appointed to the bench, and the lawyers claimed that he was biased. However, the superior court of Alameda County, which reviewed the case, disagreed. At the hearing, Warren himself answered charges of carrying out too aggressive an investigation and denied accusations that he was biased against the union.

Although Warren succeeded in fending off the legal challenges regarding his handling of this case and the negative publicity orchestrated by the union, questions about his conduct remained open in public opinion. Warren himself clearly had second thoughts—if not at the time of the trial, then years later. During his term as chief justice, the Supreme Court was asked to rule on numerous cases involving the rights of accused criminals. Warren assumed a leading role in establishing procedural safeguards based on specific constitutional provisions.

Ironically, several years before the *Point Lobos* case, Warren had recognized the need to provide professional training to law enforcement officers. Up to that time, few provisions had been made to educate policemen, to permit—let alone encourage—cooperation among forces from neighboring municipalities, or to prevent corruption among police officers. In the early 1930s, while serving as chairman of the Board of Managers for the California Bureau of Criminal Identification and Investigation, Warren initiated certain necessary reforms.

The board also came up with the idea of establishing a police-training program, to be held at the local San Jose State University. The program's faculty consisted of outstanding police officers, laboratory technicians, prosecuting attorneys, and an agent from the Federal Bureau of Investigation. Many participants, eager to obtain professional training, offered to pay their own way or use their vacations to attend. By giving the officers a sense of professionalism and providing valuable instruction from experts, the program boosted morale among the forces and increased their effectiveness on the job.

Despite his tough stand in dealing with defendants, Warren demonstrated respect for the rights of accused criminals in other contexts, and worked to extend those rights to all members of the community. For example, he helped to establish a Legal Aid Bureau in Oakland to assist poor people involved in civil cases, and he supported a county charter provision that assigned lawyers to those who could not otherwise afford legal counsel. He also attempted, unsuccessfully, to initiate for changes in the juvenile justice system. Rather than turning young offenders over to the courts, he argued that juvenile court commissioners should be appointed to "work with a patient and sociological viewpoint rather than a strictly legal one." He supported the establishment of minimum security prisons, without bars or armed guards, where nonviolent prisoners raised vegetables for county hospitals or carried out other unskilled but useful tasks. This system later became a national model.

Warren earned a reputation as a tough but fair-minded prosecutor. In 1931, Raymond Moley, a professor of public law at Columbia University who later became one of President Franklin D. Roosevelt's advisors, announced after conducting a survey of district attorneys that Warren was "the most intelligent and politically independent district attorney in the United States."

At the same time that Warren's professional responsibilities were attracting national attention, his own family responsibilities were demanding more of his time and energy. By 1935, the family had grown to include Virginia, Earl Jr., Dorothy, Nina Elisabeth, and Robert. Earl and Nina purchased their first home that year, a rather grand, furnished, three-story house in Oakland. It had a paneled study on the third floor; seven bedrooms; a parlor and a solarium; kitchen, breakfast, and dining rooms; and a front lawn big enough for touch football.

As had his own father, Earl instilled in his children a respect for education and provided a model of life-long learning for them to follow. In the evenings, he helped his children with their homework, often debating issues with them in order to teach them to think carefully and defend their positions. Occasionally accompanied by one of his children he visited a local bookstore in downtown Oakland.

Both parents expected their children to work hard, though grades were not the measure of success, reflecting Warren's personal attitude toward formal education. James, whom Warren had adopted when he married Nina, later observed that *"slacker* was a big word when I was a kid. ...Give, give, give—all you've got—to whatever it is you want to be." The Warrens encouraged their children to participate in sports and other extracurricular activities, and showed their support by attending swimming meets, riding competitions, music recitals, and scouting ceremonies whenever possible. They also urged both the boys and the girls to learn practical skills, such as carpentry—useful abilities that Earl himself had lacked.

To teach lessons of right and wrong, Earl and Nina resorted to reason rather than physical punishment. To convey the importance of self-discipline, they allowed their children a good deal of independence but also made it clear that once a decision was made, it should be seen through to completion.

Although the Warren children felt a good deal of pressure to excel, they also enjoyed special holiday celebrations and, when they were small, weekly adventures with their father. At Christmas, for example, each child had his or her own tree, surrounded by presents. And to give his wife an occasional break, Warren planned weekend outings that began after the children attended Sunday school at the local Baptist Church (he considered himself a Methodist but did not attend church). Warren later confessed that "we got to every amusement place around Oakland. . . . I've ridden thousands of miles on merry-go-rounds. It was a lot of fun, but before the day was over it could be wearing, and made me appreciate my wife more than ever." Warren was determined to maintain a sharp separation between the private and public spheres of life. Not until he entered state politics did he permit his family to appear in public for political purposes. When he finally agreed to allow photographs and make public appearances, his family's "all-American" image greatly enhanced his popular appeal as a candidate.

# Elect...

# EARL
# WARREN

## Your Next

## ATTORNEY
## GENERAL

◆

Candidate for Republican, Democratic and
Progressive Nominations

◆

*"My one desire as Attorney General would be
to contribute my part toward making California a happier and safer place in which to live"*

*Warren ran on all three major party tickets when he campaigned for the office of California attorney
general in 1938. The Progressives had adopted this strategy when Hiram Johnson was the party leader
in the early years of the 20th century, and Warren carried on the tradition even though he was officially aligned with the Republican Party.*

3

# WARTIME DECISIONS

During the 1930s, Earl Warren became actively involved in Republican party politics. He chose to align himself with the Republicans for practical as well as ideological reasons. As he explained in his memoirs, Republicans had dominated California politics since the early 20th century; "the only real division was determined by whether Republicans favored the Hiram Johnson reform wing of the party or the 'Old Guard.'"

In the 1934 elections, Warren, who was chairman of the Republican State Central Committee, proposed several amendments to the California constitution that would radically change the office of state attorney general. He was motivated by his interest in running for the office and his realization that he could not afford to serve as attorney general unless it became a full-time position. He was also concerned that the powers of the attorney general's office were not clearly defined.

The incumbent, Ulysses S. Webb, had been in office since 1902 and was paid only $5,000 a year, a salary set by the California constitution. He supplemented his income by engaging in private legal practice, as did his deputies, who earned just $3,000 annually. It seemed to Warren and others that this part-time approach to the state's legal administration created the potential for a conflict of interest. For example, the attorney general's private practice might conflict with his public responsibilities and, as a result, interfere with the efficient operation of the judicial system.

The amendments raised the attorney general's annual salary to $11,000 and established a Department of Justice; California became the first state to have one. The new statutes also empowered the attorney general to oversee all the state's local and county law enforcement agencies and to supervise all other state agencies that were involved with law enforcement.

Because of the job's increased responsibilities, Webb decided to retire in 1938. On February 17 of that year, Warren declared his candidacy for state attorney general, asserting that his 13 years as district attorney had "not only acquainted" him with the great problems of law enforcement challenging the state but had also given him "the sincere desire to strive for their solution." Under the reforms that Hiram Johnson had proposed, candidates could "cross over," or run for the nomination of more than one party. Warren, therefore, registered for all three primaries: Democratic, Progressive, and Republican. Confident that he would win most Republicans' votes, he aimed his campaign at Democrats.

In the midst of the primary race, on May 14, 1938, Warren's father was murdered in his home in Bakersfield. Warren flew to Bakersfield that evening and the following morning met with reporters in his hotel room. Overcome by grief, the attorney general broke into tears. One photographer took advantage of the moment and took a picture of Warren crying, but the other reporters grabbed the camera and exposed the film to the light. As an observer later explained, "We all felt that Warren was such a decent guy that [we] wanted to protect him."

Despite the fact that he lacked jurisdiction in Kern County, where Bakersfield is located, Warren sent staff from his Oakland office to oversee the investigation and ensure that the rights of the accused were respected. He was apparently concerned that local officials, in their eagerness to identify the murderer, might ignore protections guaranteed under the Constitution. More than 100 suspects were questioned and several were held, but all were eventually released for lack of evidence. After several months, Warren's chief inspector, Oscar Jahnsen, believed that he had found the murderer, but before he had a chance to conduct his own questioning the local authorities intervened. When the suspect's lawyer learned that the police were giving his client the third degree, or an intensive questioning, he advised his client to remain silent. The man was later released because of a lack of evidence. In the end, charges for Methias Warren's murder were never brought.

In the meantime, Warren won all three primaries and, by a margin of more than 2 million votes, the general election in November. As a result, he became the only major Republican to survive the Democratic landslide in the 1938 California elections; this reflected the fact that, though he called himself a Republican, he supported Franklin D. Roosevelt's New Deal program and was moving closer to the liberal end of the political spectrum.

Warren's uncompromising ethical standards immediately became apparent in his plan to reorganize the office of attorney general. He replaced employees who had been appointed for political reasons with a team of 50 attorneys and investigators selected on the basis of their professional qualifications, and he established rules prohibiting them from maintaining private law practices. As a manager he earned the respect of his staff and associates. "The Chief," a close advisor commented during an interview many years later, "was a demanding man for whom to work. He was a perfectionist who treated his staff fairly. He gave all of us a wide latitude and responsibility." A young clerk in the office remembered Warren as being "rather intimidating," and friendly but reserved.

Influenced not only by the harm he saw being done to individuals and their families but also by the threat that organized crime could gain a stronghold in the state, Warren was determined to end illegal gambling, from dog tracks to offshore casinos. Using a direct, no-nonsense approach, he convinced dog-track operators around the state to close down their operations so as to avoid facing prosecution.

Closing down offshore gambling ships took a good deal more work, however. Four casinos operated off the coast of Santa Monica and Long Beach, near Los Angeles. Because of the configuration of the local harbors, the shipowners maintained that the casinos were beyond the three-mile limit within which the state had jurisdiction. Warren decided otherwise but had little local support for his efforts: Los Angeles newspapers cooperated with the gambling ships, running full-page advertisements on a daily basis, and the local police departments refused to confront the shipowners.

As a first step, Warren sent his chief inspector, Oscar Jahnsen, to confer with Tony Cornero, owner of the casino ship *Rex*. Cornero had a reputation for being associated with organized crime—particularly with Al Capone, the infamous Chicago bootlegger and gangster—and during Prohibition he had been a notorious rumrunner. Cornero was unwilling to bargain with the attorney general or his associates. Consequently, Warren Olney, the assistant attorney general in charge of the operation, made plans to raid all four ships at once. With the cooperation of the Coast Guard and, after a good deal of arm twisting, the assistance of local law enforcement, Olney assembled a fleet of boats and about 300 men to carry out the raid. The crew of the *Rex* held out the longest but gave up after several hours. Defeated, Cornero was forced to bear the cost of the police action, which ran to more than $13,000, and to turn over his ship to the government in payment of more than $100,000 he owed in federal taxes, along with $4,200 he had made from the gambling operations.

Warren's achievements in law enforcement were, he believed, being threatened by the meddling of Governor Culbert L. Olson, a New Deal Democrat who had begun his career as a Progressive but had shifted his allegiance to Franklin D. Roosevelt in the early years of the Great Depression. Warren as attorney general objected when the governor interfered in matters that he considered under his own jurisdiction, and he questioned a number of Olson's decisions relating to law enforcement that Warren thought were politically motivated. The governor, in turn, apparently believed that challenging Warren's authority would enhance his own political status and discredit his rival.

Over time, tensions mounted. Warren, for example, was furious when Olson pardoned Tom Mooney, a militant labor advocate who had been convicted of planting a bomb during a parade in July 1916 that had resulted in 10 deaths. President Woodrow Wilson had commuted Mooney's death sentence to life imprisonment, but Olson decided to take the case a step further by insisting that Mooney had been framed and granting an unconditional pardon. Warren suspected that Olson was hoping to strengthen his popularity among union members by overlooking Mooney's violent tactics. However, regardless of Olson's motivation for the pardon, Warren's chief concern was that the governor's action would be interpreted as undermining law enforcement and, on that basis, Warren challenged not Olson's right to grant the pardon but his wisdom in exercising that right in this case.

Warren was even angrier when Olson decided to intervene on behalf of the men convicted of the *Point Lobos* murder. Accompanied by the press, in 1940 the governor visited San Quentin prison and determined that in his judgment the men convicted of the crime were not "the type of men who would deliberately participate in the murder of anyone." Olson hit a nerve with Warren when he picked up on questions that had been raised at the time of the trial and charged that some of the evidence had been "conflicting and impeached," or in other words questionable. Warren felt this to be an attack on his personal integrity and deeply resented the governor's intervention, a year after the trial, to secure parole for the men involved.

The most serious clash between governor and attorney general involved state preparations for civil defense. Beginning in 1939, with the outbreak of World War II in Europe, both men claimed responsibility for establishing and administering programs to defend California against any possible emergency or disaster.

On December 14, 1941, just a week after the Japanese bombing of Pearl Harbor, Hawaii, that precipitated U.S. entry into World War II, Governor Olson declared a state of emergency and assumed the primary responsibility for the state's civil defense. Warren challenged the constitutionality of this action, citing a 1929 state law that prohibited the governor from assuming emergency powers in time of war. Angered, Olson refused to recognize Warren in council meetings, share information regarding plans for civil defense, or approve appropriations of $214,000 to meet war-related expenses of the attorney general's office, including a plan to prevent the sabotaging of defense industries involved in the construction of airplanes and ships. In response to this treatment, Warren decided to challenge Olson in the next election. In April 1942, he announced his intent to run for governor.

While these cat-and-mouse games were catching the attention of state politicians, at the national level Warren was becoming known for urging the internment, or confinement, of Japanese immigrants and Americans of Japanese descent. Already engaged in planning for civil defense, Attorney General Warren was ready to take one more step to ensure the safety of the community—in this case the removal of Japanese Americans from their homes to relocation camps.

Not until after he had retired from the Supreme Court did Warren publicly acknowledge that his support of internment had been a mistake. When interviewed in 1972 he commented, "I feel that everybody who had anything to do with the relocation of the Japanese, after it was all over, had something of a guilty conscience about it, and wanted to show that it wasn't a racial thing as much as it was a defense matter." Warren nevertheless took responsibility for his own role: "I have since deeply regretted the removal order and my own testimony advocating it, because it was not in keeping with our American concept of freedom and the rights of citizens. Whenever I thought of the innocent little children who were torn from home, school friends, and congenial surroundings, I was conscience-stricken." As he concluded in his memoirs, "It was wrong to react so impulsively, without positive evidence of disloyalty, even though we felt we had a good motive in the security of our state."

Immediately after the attack on Pearl Harbor, President Roosevelt appointed a commission chaired by Supreme Court Justice Owen J. Roberts to investigate the bombing. The commission claimed to find evidence of a highly organized conspiracy:

> It has been discovered that the Japanese consul sent to and received from Tokyo in his own and other names many messages on commercial radio circuits. This greatly increased towards December 7, 1941.... [The Japanese] knew from maps which they had obtained, the exact location of vital air fields, hangars, and other structures. They also knew accurately where certain important naval vessels would be berthed. Their fliers had the most detailed maps, course, and bearings, so that each could attack a given vessel or field. Each seems to have been given a special mission.

This report, later disclaimed by the military, resulted in press headlines that misled politicians and the public.

General John L. DeWitt, commander of the U.S. troops on the West Coast, initially rejected proposals to move all

*Issei* (Japanese immigrants) and *Nisei* (native-born Americans of Japanese descent) to relocation camps. He was confident that the army could identify disloyal individuals and deal with them accordingly. Despite reports submitted by army units as well as civilians that Japanese Americans had carried out a variety of activities helpful to the enemy—from cutting power lines to planting tomatoes in patterns that directed Japanese planes toward critical targets to sending short-wave radio transmissions to Japanese submarines off the California coast—intelligence officers were unable to substantiate a single report of espionage or sabotage.

The lack of verifiable evidence would normally have defused any discussion of internment, but these were not normal times, and faulty logic prevailed. Warren, like others, interpreted the lack of evidence as threatening. He reasoned that intelligence officers had detected no evidence of espionage or sabotage before the attack on Pearl Harbor and, therefore, the absence of such evidence following the attack should also be regarded as ominous.

General DeWitt began to waver in his resistance to internment after meeting with Governor Olson and Attorney General Warren in January 1942. Californians, he had learned "feel that they are living in the midst of a lot of enemies." This perception was reinforced by a report from one of his subordinates, Colonel Karl Bendetsen, assigned to assist DeWitt in making a final recommendation. Bendetsen, a Stanford Law graduate, failed to find military justification for the internment proposal but nevertheless concluded that the loyalty of both *Issei* and *Nisei* was inherently suspect.

DeWitt's decision ultimately to support relocation persuaded key officials in Washington, D.C., to change their positions as well. Attorney General Francis Biddle, Secretary of War Henry L. Stimson, and Assistant Secretary of the Navy John J. McCloy had initially opposed internment as a violation of individual rights. On assuming his position in the cabinet, Biddle had declared: "The most important job

an Attorney General can do in time of emergency is to protect civil liberties.... Civil liberties are the essence of the
democracy we are pledged to protect." Despite this commitment, Biddle was unable to hold out against pressures
from leading journalists, aroused public opinion, and the
lobbying of West Coast politicians—governors, attorneys
general, and congressional representatives from Washington,
Oregon, and California—particularly when combined with
DeWitt's own recommendation in favor of relocation.

Stimson also gave in under pressure, as did McCloy.
The secretary of war, writing in 1947, explained that
"Japanese raids on the west coast seemed not only possible
but probable in the first months of the war, and it was quite
impossible to be sure that the raiders would not receive
important help from individuals from Japanese origin." Like
Warren, these leaders were content to rely on speculation
rather than hard evidence.

President Roosevelt, Stimson said, "was very vigorous"
about the proposal to relocate the Japanese Americans.
Biddle observed, "I do not think [Roosevelt] was much
concerned with the gravity or implications of this step....
Nor do I think that the constitutional difficulty plagued
him—the Constitution has never greatly bothered any
wartime President. That was a question of law, which ultimately the Supreme Court must decide."

On February 19, 1942, President Roosevelt signed
Executive Order 9066, which gave the secretary of war
authority to identify militarily sensitive regions and exclude
from those areas individuals and groups considered a national
security threat. Two days later, Warren testified before the
House Committee on National Defense Migration. In his
remarks, he distinguished between Americans of Caucasian
background and those of Asian descent. He assumed that,
unlike immigrants from Europe, who he believed gave up
their former loyalties when they settled in the United States,
the Japanese clung to their ethnic and racial identities.

By this time, Warren had shifted from his original position, that only Japanese aliens—people who had been born in Japan and had emigrated to the United States—should be relocated, to one that called for the relocation of all Japanese Americans. Warren was not alone, but his voice was among the most influential. He was, after all, the principal law enforcement officer in a politically significant state. By a unanimous vote, Congress passed a law on March 19 imposing penalties of one year in prison and a $5,000 fine for those who refused to obey the policy of internment.

The government first imposed a curfew on ethnic Japanese, requiring them to remain indoors from 8 P.M. to 6 A.M. It then ordered both *Issei* and *Nisei* to report to "assembly centers," allowing them between seven and ten days to sell their homes, most of their possessions, and their businesses. They were then assigned to one of ten camps scattered throughout the country—three of them in California—where they remained behind barbed-wire fences for up to four years. In all, more than 110,000 Japanese immigrants and Americans of Japanese descent spent most of the war in these internment camps. Not until 1988 did the U.S. government make an attempt at amends. At that time, Congress passed the Civil Liberties Act, authorizing a formal Presidential apology and payment of $20,000 to each of the 82,219 former internees who were still alive or the immediate families of those deceased.

Racism was clearly a factor influencing the government's policy of Japanese internment. Although the United States was fighting at the same time against Germany and Italy, officials—including Warren—did not propose relocating German Americans and Italian Americans. These groups, policymakers argued, did not live in isolated communities as did the Japanese Americans and were therefore considered less attached to their homelands and consequently less likely to conspire against the United States. What these officials

failed to acknowledge was that it was precisely the existence of certain state and federal restrictions, including laws that prevented Japanese immigrants from becoming citizens or owning land, that were largely responsible for the segregation of Japanese Americans from the rest of the society.

Warren claimed in his memoirs that "I have always believed that I had no prejudice against the Japanese as such except that directly spawned by Pearl Harbor and its aftermath." He had certainly had many opportunities to examine his own thinking on this subject—as a youngster in Bakersfield, where discrimination against Asians was public policy, and as an aspiring politician in a state where anti-Asian attitudes were common among those who called themselves Progressives.

Following the examples set by his predecessors Hiram Johnson and Ulysses S. Webb, Warren had joined the Native Sons of the Golden West when he was district attorney of

*Japanese-American women at a temporary detention camp in Santa Anita are busy doing laundry for their families. The federal government ordered both immigrants and native-born Americans of Japanese descent to "relocation centers," where they remained until the Supreme Court finally ruled in 1945 that detention was unconstitutional.*

Alameda County. This organization had been founded in 1875, and by the turn of the century it had 200 branches throughout California and the West. From that time until the beginning of the Great Depression, it was one of the most influential pressure groups in California. Its monthly publication, *The Grizzly Bear,* warned repeatedly of what it called "the Asiatic Peril" and routinely supported the segregation of white and Asian students in the public schools and the exclusion of Japanese immigrants from the western states.

In the years directly following World War I, the Native Sons joined with the Native Daughters of the Golden West, the American Legion, the California State Federation of Labor, and the state's two largest farm groups—the Farm Bureau and the State Grange—to further its anti-Japanese agenda. Members of the Native Sons, including Attorney General Webb, testified in U.S. Senate hearings to restrict immigration. The resultant legislation, the National Origins Quota Act of 1924, sharply limited the number of immigrants from southern and eastern Europe and completely excluded all East Asians. After the attack on Pearl Harbor, the Native Sons actively supported the relocation of Japanese Americans. In June 1942, the organization filed a lawsuit intended to deny citizenship to all Japanese Americans, but the 9th Circuit Court of Appeals rejected their argument.

Warren's decision to join this organization may have been part of a larger strategy to establish a political base through memberships in civic and fraternal organizations. Even if this were the explanation, his membership suggests either a willingness to place political advantage over ethical considerations or a disregard for the racist agenda associated with the organization. In either case, his affiliation with this group conveyed an endorsement of racist sentiments that Warren would later regret.

In contrast, Warren's championing of a civil case involving the rights of Native Americans better reflects the genuine humanity and sense of justice that came to characterize him later in his life. The U.S. government had drafted treaties in 1851 and 1852, in the aftermath of the gold rush, to reimburse the Indians at the rate of 50 cents per acre for land that had been taken by prospectors and settlers. The U.S. Senate had never ratified the document, however, and the federal government never followed through on its part of the bargain. Approached by a delegation of Native Americans, Warren quickly recognized the justice of their cause and agreed to pursue their case. As a result of his efforts, descendants of the Indians who had lived in California in the mid-19th century—"wandering bands, tribes, and small groups, who had been roving over the same territory during the period under Spanish and Mexican ownership"—were awarded more than $7 million, or about $350 per person, by the federal government.

During Warren's term as California's attorney general, his office prepared approximately 3,000 advisory opinions for the Olson administration and state legislative officials, was involved in nearly 500 criminal prosecutions, and argued 25 cases before the U.S. Supreme Court. In 1940, Warren was elected president of the National Association of Attorneys General. By the time he entered the race for governor of California on April 10, 1942, he had a strong record of public service and had established a national reputation for his work in the field of law enforcement and as a leader within the Republican Party.

Following a Progressive strategy, Warren ran in both the Republican and Democratic primaries and adopted a nonpartisan position that allowed him to support President Roosevelt's popular New Deal domestic programs and to pledge his "unqualified support in prosecuting the war." This strategy alienated conservatives, including the wealthy businessmen Warren had counted on to finance his campaign, but it strengthened his popularity among moderates and liberals. In the long run, Warren benefited from the fact that he received no money from special interests. His financial independence made his claim to represent the people more believable.

Governor Olson campaigned in the big cities and relied heavily on radio speeches. He claimed credit for the state's economic prosperity, which was in fact a product of wartime production in the defense industries, and reminded voters of his efforts to promote social welfare legislation, including state medical insurance. With the exception of the Sailors' Union of the Pacific and a few small unions, organized labor officially endorsed the Democratic governor.

Warren, in contrast, attempted to make personal contact with as many voters as possible. He visited the smaller cities surrounding Los Angeles, San Francisco, and Oakland and campaigned in rural parts of the state. Traveling by car with his former army pal, Leo Carillo—"The Cisco Kid" from the movies—Warren crisscrossed the state, stopping to talk to workers at airplane factories and shipyards, in fruit fields and small towns, oil refineries and mining camps. The main theme of his campaign was the need to plan for the future. He was convinced that the state would continue to

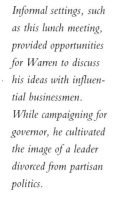

*Informal settings, such as this lunch meeting, provided opportunities for Warren to discuss his ideas with influential businessmen. While campaigning for governor, he cultivated the image of a leader divorced from partisan politics.*

grow. Government, he argued, needed to anticipate rather than react to that growth. California needed to plan ahead: establish a sound financial policy, conserve natural resources, develop a water supply, expand its highway system, improve public education, and provide for adequate law enforcement. The state also had to become more responsive to the needs of its people, ensuring their financial security through old-age pensions.

The major newspapers in the state, including those with Democratic ties, supported Warren. The *Los Angeles Times, San Francisco Chronicle,* and *Oakland Tribune* all backed the attorney general. Working with professional campaign advisors, Warren changed his image from that of a no-nonsense public attorney to that of a family man deeply committed to his wife and children. Campaign advertisements pictured the smiling candidate surrounded by wholesome and happy family members.

The campaign was a great success. By distancing himself from special interests—wealthy businessmen, professional politicians, and labor unions—and presenting himself as a candidate committed to the interests of the individual, Warren convinced voters to cast their ballots for him. In addition to winning the Republican primary, he received 404,778 votes in the Democratic primary, as compared to 514,144 votes cast for Olson. His 335,000 majority in the November elections—Warren won every county in the state but one—represented a clear mandate for "Leadership, Not Politics."

# 4

# GOVERNING CALIFORNIA: "FIRST THINGS FIRST"

Earl Warren's family was an important political as well as personal asset throughout his three terms as governor. Earl Jr. and Robert usually stayed home during electoral campaigns, but Virginia, Dorothy, and Nina Elisabeth (nicknamed "Honey Bear") enjoyed posing for photographs and making public appearances with their father.

Beginning in 1944, the so-called family magazines *Life, Better Homes and Gardens, Redbook,* and the *Saturday Evening Post* published illustrated articles about the Warrens, emphasizing the "all-American" qualities that made the family so appealing to readers. For example, a *Life* Magazine article observed that "appropriately in a Republican family all the Warrens are individualists, each with his own idea of how to get the most out of life. . . . Collectively, the Warrens share happy dispositions, unself-consciousness and violently good health."

Virginia was 14 when her father took the oath of office as governor on January 3, 1943; Bobby was just seven. Warren recalled in his memoirs that 12-year-old Earl Jr., when asked by journalists which of the speeches he had liked best, responded, "I believe I liked the lieutenant governor's best.

*The Warrens—Bobby, Nina Elisabeth (Honey Bear), Dottie, Earl Jr., Virginia, Jim, Nina, and Earl—demonstrate family solidarity during the gubernatorial campaign of 1942. This public relations photograph was taken at the Warrens' home on Vernon Street in Oakland.*

It was shorter. You know in a warm room like that people don't listen well to a long speech."

Though it was not particularly long by adult standards, Warren's inaugural speech lasted 40 minutes. In it he established the ground rules for his administration and offered a preview of his legislative agenda. "Let's cut out all the dry rot of petty politics, partisan jockeying, inaction, dictatorial stubbornness and opportunistic thinking," he declared. "Let's do first things first."

The theme of nonpartisan government, especially in time of war, was not just talk. Warren still adhered to the core elements of the Progressive Party's platform: honesty and openness in government, opposition to powerful interest groups, and concern for public opinion. However, his agenda gradually came to reflect a liberal attitude toward government. Despite opposition from conservative groups in California, Warren insisted that government play a more active role in providing for individual and social welfare. He worked to improve the quality of health care, opportunities for education, and protections for working people, and to provide better treatment of prisoners.

Above all, Warren considered himself a pragmatist. His overall strategy was to identify needs and problems, talk to knowledgeable people, read extensively about the issues, enlist the help of experts, develop proposals based on their recommendations, persuade the public to support these measures, and then to urge members of the state legislature to enact laws to implement his programs.

Rather than allowing a party platform to dictate the agenda, Warren developed his own program, based on professional experience and personal insights. Many of his proposals, such as expansion of the highway system, extension of the university system, and provisions to fund public schools, were part of his master plan to deal with population growth. Others, such as state health insurance, resulted from firsthand experience. After being hospitalized for several weeks during his first term as governor, Warren realized that most families could not afford the costs of long-term illness.

Determined to govern for the common good, Warren refused to grant privileges to powerful individuals or organizations. From his first day on the job, he made it clear that all business would be transacted through the front door. Any individual who wanted to meet with him had to make an appointment at the office and have his name posted on the bulletin board there so that the press could keep track of who was talking to the governor. This policy helped discourage lobbyists who wanted to exercise influence secretly.

In order to share his ideas with the public and find out what his constituents thought about certain issues, the governor instituted "town hall" meetings, held in the capital, Sacramento, but open to citizens from around the state. These conferences were generally two or three days long and attracted between 1,000 and 3,000 participants, each paying his or her own expenses and representing a variety of viewpoints. Warren introduced the topics to be considered—such as public health, highway expansion, water supply, conservation, prison reform, employment, juvenile delinquency, old-age pensions, and so on—and then the participants divided up into groups to discuss the issues. Each of the 20 or so groups prepared summaries of their discussions that were then incorporated into conference reports that in turn became the basis for legislation.

Both the availability and the quality of health care emerged as major items on Warren's agenda. Because the need for medical facilities was not contested, Warren did not have to persuade the public or their elected representatives to improve existing hospitals or build new hospitals where none existed. Nor did he have to fight to establish a more humane system for helping individuals diagnosed as mentally ill. Armed with reports from safety inspectors and health professionals, the administration secured the necessary funding for the successful implementation of its health-care program. The key components of the program were building hospitals in rural areas and upgrading existing facilities to attract well-qualified physicians.

In contrast, the governor's efforts to establish a program for state health insurance met with strong opposition, demonstrating the enormous power that special-interest groups wielded in state politics. Warren announced his plan in January 1945. Aimed at workers who earned $2,500 a year or less (about $24,500 in today's dollars)—two-thirds of all workers and their families—it would have covered doctors' fees, laboratory and X-ray charges, medicines, some dental services, and 21 days of hospitalization. The only compulsory component was funding: employers and employees would have shared a 3 percent payroll tax to cover the costs of administration and care. Patients would have been allowed to select their own physicians, and doctors could have chosen not to provide their services through the program.

The governor expected little opposition, but he was wrong. The California Medical Association (CMA) quickly denounced the plan as socialized medicine (medical care funded by the government), and launched an aggressive advertising campaign to ensure its defeat. Nine thousand physicians around the state attacked the proposal, claiming that it would force doctors to become state employees and bring an end to private medical practice. The bill was defeated.

Willing to compromise, Warren proposed payroll deductions to pay for hospital insurance, but the CMA viewed this measure as a subterfuge, a first step toward the more comprehensive proposal it had just succeeded in killing. A second compromise, supported by Warren and sponsored by organized labor, eventually passed. It expanded medical insurance coverage for workers to include illnesses not related to their jobs, but did not cover all medical costs for working families.

As governor, Warren remained committed to improving law enforcement and the treatment of prisoners. The restructuring of California's corrections system was linked in his mind to his goal of social justice and his belief that government can be a positive force for change. In 1944, he called a special session of the legislature to deal with prison reform. His goal was to create a Department of Corrections, which would centralize authority, develop new facilities, and oversee the implementation of programs. With the cooperation of lawmakers, the Prison Re-organization Act passed and went into effect on May 1. The new department included three main units: a Youth Authority, an Adult Authority, and a Women's Prison Board.

Warren was particularly disturbed by statistics that showed a disproportionate number of crimes being committed by juvenile offenders. Youths between the ages of 13 and 21 constituted only 13 percent of the population but were responsible for 40 percent of serious crime. In absolute numbers, more than 50,000 young people were arrested in California in a single year and 22,000 were brought to court. Consequently, the Youth Authority, headed by Warren's college friend Walter Gordon, took on the task of devising strategies in place of punishment to help young people acquire education and training that would allow them to become productive members of society. Under Gordon, the authority also developed the Delinquency Prevention Program.

At the most basic level, prisoners benefited from new facilities, better food, educational opportunities, and vocational training programs. Reforms brought an end to the long-standing practice of using the toughest criminals—often bullies—to keep order in prisons, and instituted professional training for the guards.

Under Warren's governance, opportunities for higher education increased throughout the state. The University of California established new campuses at Riverside and Santa Barbara and enlarged its branches in Davis and Los Angeles. California's state university system was also expanded. With the addition of three new colleges, in Long Beach, Los Angeles, and Sacramento, the state university system now included 11 campuses enrolling 380,000 students. The junior college system also grew, providing places for 74,000 students on 77 campuses.

Warren's record on civil liberties was mixed. As governor, he was the ex officio chairman of the Board of Regents of the University of California and thus found himself drawn into a battle involving academic freedom. The trouble began in January 1949, in the early years of the cold war. Convinced that communists presented a serious threat, lawmakers at both the state and federal levels of government had begun adopting measures designed to protect the country from the perceived dangers.

A bill was introduced to give the California legislature the authority to determine whether University of California employees were communist sympathizers. When the U.C. Berkeley president, Robert Gordon Sproul, learned of the proposal, he decided to act before the legislature had a chance to proceed with passage of the bill. On March 25, 1949, he recommended to the regents that faculty be required to swear that they did not support "any party or

organization that believes in, advocates, or teaches the overthrow of the United States government by force or violence."
The faculty members learned about the oaths in May.

The regents insisted that they had the authority to
establish and enforce such university policies. The faculty
argued instead that they had the right to hold or express
their own views without fear of arbitrary interference by
officials. Unable to work out a compromise, Sproul asked
Warren to attend upcoming meetings of the regents. The
governor was a loyal alumnus with strong ties to the university and therefore was prepared to do whatever he could to
break the stalemate. Satisfied with policies adopted in 1940
that prevented the university from hiring communists, the
governor helped to reach a compromise that replaced the
sworn oath with a simple statement denying membership in
the Communist Party or any other organization advocating
overthrow of the government by force or violence. The
statement, unlike the oath, would not subject a person to
prosecution for perjury if it were false.

In October 1950, Warren appeared to change course
entirely when he signed the Levering Act, which required
all state employees, including university faculty, to sign an
oath stating that they did not support the Communist Party.
He attempted to justify this shift by classifying the Levering
Act as a wartime measure; the United States had been fighting communist forces in Korea since early summer.

In other areas, Warren's record was equally mixed. Even
with the first tax reduction in California's history, Warren
was able to balance the state's budget and build a reserve of
$43 million needed for post–World War II restructuring.
The peacetime return of 850,000 servicemen to California
along with approximately 110,000 Japanese Americans from
the internment camps raised the cost of housing until the
legislature, with Warren's approval, established rent controls.
He increased old-age pensions from $40 to $50 per month,
made unemployment benefits available for the first time to

employees of smaller businesses, and increased compensation for workers injured on the job, raised the minimum pay for teachers, and opened child-care facilities. Concerned with preserving natural resources and the environment, he set aside additional lands for parks and recreation.

In the civil rights arena, Warren was unable to persuade the legislature to adopt his Fair Employment Practices Act, a bill intended to reduce discrimination against minorities and women in the workplace. However, he integrated the California National Guard shortly after World War II, assured minorities of equal employment opportunities in the state civil service, and appointed several African-American judges to the state courts. When Japanese Americans returned from the internment camps in 1945, he openly defended their right to live wherever they chose, provided police protection during the resettlement process, and refused to appeal a federal court decision ending segregation of Native American and Asian children in California schools.

Warren's increasing popularity among California voters drew the attention of national politicians. In 1944, he turned down the Republication nomination for Vice President because he was certain that Americans would elect Franklin

Governor Warren signed a state law compensating Americans of Japanese ancestry for the losses they suffered as a result of relocation. As governor, he attempted to make amends for the treatment of Japanese Americans, which he had supported, during World War II.

Roosevelt to a fourth term, and they did. But four years later he was ready to reconsider.

By May 1947, he had begun to think about running for the Presidency. He accepted an invitation to speak at the Gridiron Club, a prestigious press association in Washington, D.C., and, within the next few months made nine trips outside California. Satisfied that he had a reasonable chance to secure the Republican Party's Presidential nomination, he agreed to run as a "favorite son"—a candidate supported by local political leaders—from California. That decision guaranteed him 53 votes at the Republican convention, but he had formidable opposition. Thomas Dewey, governor of New York and the Republican Presidential candidate in 1944, was the leading contender. Senators Robert A. Taft and Arthur H. Vandenberg, General Douglas MacArthur, and former Minnesota governor Harold Stassen each had enough supporters to influence the voting. Warren's only hope was for a deadlock, at which point he could emerge as a compromise candidate.

Once it became apparent that Dewey was the frontrunner, Warren released his claim on the California delegates and the convention nominated Dewey for the second time. The New Yorker invited Warren to become his running mate. Despite the view of the Republican leadership—party national chairman Hugh Scott claimed they had put together "a dreamboat of a ticket"—Warren had serious reservations from the start. Nationwide, the press referred to the Dewey campaign as being tailor-made. "It was indeed tailor-made," Warren remarked in his memoirs, "but tailored to fit people of

*New York governor Thomas E. Dewey invited Warren to visit his dairy farm in Pawling during the 1948 campaign. Although the men were tromping through cow barns, the protocol of the time required that they wear shirt and tie whenever they appeared before the press or the public.*

any age, any size, any place, under any circumstances. Naturally, it didn't fit snugly for most. On the other hand, [Dewey's] Democratic rival, President Truman, went out to talk with the people about issues they were interested in."

Warren refused to rely on the speeches supplied by Dewey's campaign managers, but he was not entirely free to speak his mind. During a month-long whistle-stop train trip through 29 states, he wrote 52 short speeches, held 24 major rallies, and conducted 5 formal press conferences. He prepared his remarks as he went along, checking with campaign headquarters and editing as directed. Restricted by Dewey's policy of making no promises and tempered by his own reluctance to attack the Democratic ticket, he failed to stir the crowds. The most dynamic interchanges during the campaign were probably the angry telephone conversations between the two mismatched candidates, wrangling over strategies and issues. Truman's victory, predicted by Nina Warren but few others, spared the nation a President and Vice President at war with one another.

In 1950 Warren won a third term as governor, defeating James Roosevelt, son of former president Franklin D. Roosevelt. Though Warren was campaigning for state office, he emphasized national and international issues, conveying the impression that what he was really interested in was the Presidency. He endorsed federal aid to education and national health insurance and talked about the emergence of the United States as a superpower.

Ironically, Warren adopted an increasingly liberal view of government while gaining national recognition as a leader within the largely conservative Republican Party. Speaking at a Lincoln Day dinner in Boston in 1952, he focused on the role of government in ensuring equality of opportunity and the need to protect individual liberties. Despite his attempt to establish a direct link between Lincoln's political philosophy and his own, Warren's insistence on social justice placed him firmly in the Democratic camp.

# WARREN ON LINCOLN

*When Warren was a contender for the Republican Presidential nomination in 1952, he was invited to deliver the annual Lincoln Day address to a political club in Boston. Warren greatly admired Lincoln and often quoted him in public speeches. In this address, he attempts to establish a link between his own political philosophy and that of the Civil War President.*

It is often difficult to appraise the great figures of history according to the standards and the problems of our own day. So many of them were creatures only of their own times....

Not so with Lincoln. His greatness lies in the fact that he was able to live by fundamental principles and to maintain a spirit applicable to all times and under all circumstances. His clear understanding of democracy and its application to mankind in his or any other day has never been better expressed than when he said: "As I would not be a slave, so I would not be a master. This expresses my idea of democracy. Whatever differs from this, to the extent of the difference is not democracy."

His practice of homely virtues, his devotion to justice and his consideration for others are the things that have made his memory not only a treasure of patriotic sentiment, but a source of practical guidance for the nation....

We need faith as Americans have needed it in every crisis in history. The faith we need is the faith to do the things that should be done for the betterment of our people—not just some of the people, but all of the people. We should not be afraid to speak of or advocate the "general welfare." Lincoln had no such fear and the Constitution says it is the fundamental purpose for which our government is formed. We should not shy away from the term "civil liberties." The Constitution was not ratified until assurance had been given that they would be guaranteed in the Bill of Rights. And Lincoln said,

"The fight must go on. The cause of liberty must not be surrendered at the end of one or even a hundred defeats." The term "social justice" is not an evil one. It comes from the Holy Bible.

"Social progress" is nothing to run from. America is the creature of social progress, a monument to its power and beauty. It has been through a process of social progress that we have grown to leadership in the world. It was Lincoln's creed, and those who confuse it with socialism today are indulging in the kind of thinking that Lincoln described as not being able to distinguish between a horse chestnut and a chestnut horse....

It must be apparent to everyone that we have not yet achieved perfection, and that as long as there are inequalities to be adjusted, unfortunates to be helped, we must maintain faith in being able to use our institutions for improving the conditions of our citizens.

# CLOSING THE DEAL: EARL WARREN BECOMES CHIEF JUSTICE

On November 14, 1951, Earl Warren declared his intention to run for the Republican Presidential nomination. Within his own party, he faced considerable opposition from right-wing leaders who recognized the huge gap between their conservative ideals and his persistent promotion of social welfare programs. Among Democrats, however, he found allies. On the day after he announced his candidacy, President Truman declared, "Governor Warren is a fine man. I once said that he was a Democrat and didn't know it." That judgment, he added, "still goes."

When he joined the national race, Warren knew that he stood only an outside chance of winning the nomination. Senator Robert A. Taft of Ohio was the leading contender until General Dwight D. Eisenhower decided to enter the race on January 7, 1952. As soon as the World War II hero declared himself a candidate, his nomination was virtually assured.

Warren did not have the time or resources to campaign aggressively, and the responsibilities of governing California restricted his travel. As a result, he entered only three state primaries: California, Oregon, and Wisconsin. He won only a half dozen delegate votes, from urban Milwaukee and Madison in Wisconsin, in addition to the 70 guaranteed to their "favorite son" by the California Republicans, who had selected him by a margin of two to one.

The California delegates traveled to Chicago for the national convention aboard the "Sacramento Special." Warren's three daughters—by now experienced campaigners—wore orange baseball caps bearing the letter W and danced with the delegates in the lounge car as the train crossed the Rocky Mountains and the Great Plains.

Although Warren began the trip with great expectations, his mood soon soured. In Denver, California Senator Richard Nixon and his political advisor Murray Chotiner boarded the train. Despite the fact that the California Republicans were legally bound to cast their votes for Warren until he officially gave up his claim, the two men spent the next day encouraging delegates to switch their allegiance to Eisenhower. When Warren realized what was going on—what he later referred to as the Great Train Robbery—he was furious.

Warren's anger increased when he arrived in Chicago and found the buses awaiting his delegation draped in banners proclaiming "Eisenhower for President." Warren blamed Nixon, who had secretly left the train one stop before Chicago, taken a car into the city, and apparently arranged for Eisenhower's campaign managers to pay for the buses that would carry the Californian delegates to their hotel.

*President Eisenhower, on Warren's left, followed through on his promise to appoint Warren to the first vacant seat on the Supreme Court in return for his support of Eisenhower's Republican Presidential nomination in 1952. Vice President Nixon, standing, endorsed the appointment of Warren in hopes of assuming leadership of the Republican Party in California.*

Eisenhower received 595 votes on the first ballot; Taft, 500; Warren, 81; Harold Stassen, who had become president of the University of Pennsylvania, 20; and General Douglas MacArthur, 10. Because Eisenhower needed just eight more votes for a majority, Warren E. Burger's decision as leader of the Minnesota delegation to turn that group's votes over to the front-runner clinched the nomination. As Warren anticipated, Eisenhower named Nixon as his running mate. After becoming President, Eisenhower also rewarded Burger for his role in securing the nomination. In 1953 he appointed the Minnesota Republican to serve as assistant attorney general for the Civil Defense division at the Justice Department, an appointment that proved a stepping-stone in Burger's path to a seat on the Supreme Court.

Later in the summer of 1952, the Democrats held their convention in Chicago and nominated Illinois Governor Adlai Stevenson to run against "Ike." Stevenson promised to "talk sense to the American people"; however, his careful analysis of important issues and eloquent speechmaking typically appealed to liberal intellectuals. Labor backed him, but he had to struggle to convince most Americans that another four years of Democratic leadership would be good for the country.

Warren was torn between loyalty to the Republican Party and a personal preference for Stevenson. When President Truman arrived in California to campaign for the Democratic ticket, the governor went out of his way to welcome him. Similarly, Warren arranged for Stevenson to speak on the steps of the state capitol, even though he himself was on the road campaigning for Eisenhower.

Although he admired Eisenhower's personal qualities, Warren had serious reservations about the general's positions on a number of important issues. He was deeply troubled that Eisenhower did not denounce Senator Joseph McCarthy, who two years earlier had launched his anticommunist attacks on State Department employees. Warren was especially upset when McCarthy accused distinguished World War II general and former secretary of state George C. Marshall of treason. He also resented Ike's attack on national health insurance and, more generally, the candidate's acceptance of a conservative platform drafted by Taft and his right-wing followers. Despite these misgivings, however, Warren agreed to campaign for Eisenhower. He covered 11 western states, supposedly presenting the general's positions but, in fact, voicing his own views on a range of subjects, from agricultural price supports to pro-union policies.

Warren's efforts may well have contributed to the margin of the Republican victory in November, but his support was not a deciding factor. As predicted, Eisenhower won by a landslide. He received 6 million more popular votes than Stevenson and defeated his opponent by a margin of 442 to 89 in the electoral college.

Unsuccessful in his own bid for the Presidency, Warren now had to decide what direction his career should take. Following the 1948 elections, he had been offered several positions in private business as well as the job of baseball commissioner. None had felt right. Now, four years later, he thought about running for a fourth term as governor but hoped that new opportunities would arise.

Shortly after the election, Eisenhower offered Warren a seat in his cabinet as secretary of labor or the interior, but with two children still in college the governor could not afford to take a cut in salary. He had something else in mind. At the convention, he had thrown his support behind Eisenhower and, in return, he had been promised a Supreme Court appointment. He decided to hold out for that assignment or something close to it.

In July 1953, Attorney General Herbert Brownell asked Warren if he would be willing to serve as solicitor general— in other words, whether he would become the principal lawyer for the U.S. government. Warren knew that Presidents often appoint potential Supreme Court justices to this position before elevating them to the bench. He recognized that as solicitor general he would be able to demonstrate his ability to practice law and would be a stronger candidate, so he accepted.

In early September, he announced his decision not to run for a fourth term as governor. Five days later, on September 8, Chief Justice Frederick M. Vinson died unexpectedly. Warren immediately realized that he was a contender for the position. He spent the following weekend reading a lengthy biography of the great 19th-century chief justice John Marshall.

Eisenhower considered a number of other men for the position, but Warren emerged as the strongest candidate. Had he been considered for the position of associate justice his credentials might not have been as strong. But because the empty seat was that of the chief justice, his administrative experience weighed heavily in his favor. Those who knew Warren were confident that he had the ability to handle not only the managerial responsibilities of the position but also disagreements among those who sat on the court.

Reviewing his record in public office, the President and the attorney general believed that Warren was a moderate Republican. They concluded from his record as district attorney and attorney general of California that he was a "law and order" man, prepared to take aggressive measures against criminals. Based on his support for Japanese internment, they thought that he was a conservative and therefore safe on social issues, particularly segregation. They knew he had a reputation for absolute honesty and integrity in private life and public service. Furthermore—and this may explain why they chose to ignore the more liberal aspects of his three terms as governor—they realized that by appointing Warren to the Supreme Court they would remove him as a possible challenger for the Presidential nomination in 1956. Senate Republican leader William Knowland and Vice President Nixon also backed Warren's appointment. Both men were eager to become leaders of the Republican Party in California, which was impossible as long as Warren held a state office.

Warren was appointed chief justice of the United States on September 27, 1953. At that time, a judicial appointee was not expected to testify before the Senate Judiciary Committee prior to the Senate's voting on his nomination and, as a result, the Senate voted to confirm the appointment without a long, contentious hearing. On October 4, Earl and Nina Warren flew to Washington, D.C., for Warren's swearing-in ceremony and the opening of the new term.

The Supreme Court, located across from the Capitol and next door to the Library of Congress, was completed in 1935. Constructed of white marble, the building resembles a Greek temple with its Corinthian columns and classical design. The words "Equal Justice under Law" appear over the main entrance. Large sculptured figures representing Justice and Authority sit on either side of the steps leading in to the building.

The main courtroom is simple but elegant. The ornate mahogany bench behind which the justices sit in high-backed black leather chairs is located at the far end of the room, just in front of a red velvet curtain through which the justices pass when they enter and leave the courtroom. Twenty-four Ionic columns are evenly spaced around the room, which is decorated with images of famous lawgivers including Moses, Solomon, Hammurabi, and Confucius on one wall Justinian, Muhammad, William Blackstone, and Chief Justice John Marshall on the opposite.

Earl and Nina Warren arrived at the Supreme Court at 10 A.M. on October 5, the first Monday in October and the first day of the new term. Just before midday, the senior associate justice—the justice who has been on the Court the longest time—Hugo L. Black administered the Constitutional oath in the justices' conference room. Only the eight associate justices attended.

Precisely at noon, the Court's marshal announced the opening of the session by pounding his gavel and proclaiming, "Oyez! Oyez! Oyez! All persons having business before

*Shortly after Warren took over as chief, he and the other justices met with President Eisenhower at the White House. Featured in this publicity photograph in the front row are William O. Douglas, Stanley Reed, Warren, Eisenhower, Hugo Black, and Felix Frankfurter, and in the back row, starting to Warren's right, Robert Jackson, Tom Clark, Sherman Minton, and Harold Burton.*

the Honorable, Supreme Court of the United States, are admonished to draw near and give their attention, for the Court is now sitting. God save the United States and this Honorable Court." After Justice Black announced the death of Chief Justice Vinson, the Clerk of the Supreme Court administered the judicial oath. Like others had before him, Warren raised his right hand and solemnly swore to "administer justice without respect to persons, and do equal right to the poor and to the rich . . . [to] faithfully and impartially discharge and perform all the duties incumbent upon [him] as Chief Justice of the United States, according to the best of [his] abilities and understanding, agreeable to the Constitution and the Laws of the United States." The marshal then escorted the new chief to his place at the center of the bench.

At the time of John Marshall's death in 1835, former President John Quincy Adams observed that the chief justice of the United States is a "station of the highest trust, of the deepest responsibility, and of influence far more extensive than that of the President of the United States." Often referred to as "first among equals," the chief justice has unique responsibilities that increase his influence and authority, yet his vote carries exactly the same weight as that of the associate justices. He is the head of the highest federal court and of the entire federal court system, which includes district courts and courts of appeal; he is, therefore, Chief Justice of the United States, not only of the Supreme Court.

The chief justice also plays a symbolic role, a personification of the rule of law and the ideal of equality under the law. Since 1797, he has administered the oath of office to the President of the United States. He presides over the Senate trial when a President has been impeached, because the Vice President, who normally leads the Senate in its deliberations, has an obvious interest in the outcome of these proceedings.

For the most part, the chief justice spends his time deciding cases. Like the other justices, the chief and his law clerks, who are recent graduates from the nation's top law schools, carefully research the cases that come before the bench. The justices review lower court decisions, read briefs submitted by the lawyers, and examine relevant precedents (previously decided cases that establish or clarify principles of law). They also analyze the issues and develop questions to ask when counsel for the parties appear before the Supreme Court. The justices study memoranda prepared by law clerks that are based on petitions from dissatisfied parties who wish to have their cases reviewed by the Supreme Court. These summarize for the justices the facts, issues, and merits of the cases and recommend what action, if any, the Court should take.

The chief justice presides over the Supreme Court's weekly conferences. At these meetings, which are attended only by members of the Court, the justices decide which cases to accept on appeal from the lower courts, discuss and cast preliminary votes on cases they have heard, determine who will draft the opinions, and cast their final votes once the opinions have been revised and approved. The chief justice leads off the discussions and serves as moderator for the deliberations. When voting with the majority, he decides who will write the opinion that will represent the Court's final view on a case, often assigning himself the task if the case is of particular importance.

The chief has administrative authority directly related to the operations of the Court. He decides whether lawyers should be given more time to prepare their cases and assigns counsel to those who cannot afford to pay for legal representation. In addition, he manages the budget for the entire federal court system and oversees the operations of the Supreme Court building. His other responsibilities include serving as chancellor of the Smithsonian Institution, a complex of museums and research centers run by the federal government. Until recent years this position was largely ceremonial. However, the chief justice now takes on a more active role, including providing advice about pending legislation and litigation affecting the institution.

For the most part, Earl Warren was well prepared for his new assignment. Lacking judicial experience, however, he asked Hugo Black to conduct the weekly conferences until he learned the Court's procedures. Given that Warren had had only a few days between his appointment and his swearing in, this arrangement seems to have been wise. Warren was able to get a feel for the routine and, in the process, become better acquainted with his colleagues.

Presidents Roosevelt and Truman had appointed the eight justices who were on the Court when Warren became chief justice. Most were New Deal Democrats with strong political connections. Ambitious, intelligent, and extremely capable, they had served the federal government in various capacities. Hugo L. Black, Harold H. Burton, and Sherman Minton had been senators. William O. Douglas had been chairman of the Securities and Exchange Commission. Felix Frankfurter had served as an advisor to Roosevelt. Only Minton had had any prior judicial experience. However, Burton, Douglas, and Frankfurter had taught law; Robert Jackson and Stanley F. Reed had been solicitors general, and both Jackson and Tom C. Clark had served as attorneys general of the United States.

During the 1940s, the Supreme Court had acquired a reputation for its members squabbling among themselves. The justices disagreed sharply over the role of the judiciary— whether the Court should take an active role in defending individuals' rights or should defer to the elected branches of government unless they found a flagrant violation of the Constitution. They also differed in their understanding of what key provisions, such as the 1st and 14th Amendments, meant and how they should be applied to cases. The combination of fundamental differences relating to their work and strong, self-centered personalities led to long-standing rivalries, sharp words, and generally unpleasant working conditions.

President Truman had selected Warren's predecessor, Frederick M. Vinson, in hopes that this mild-mannered southerner could restore harmony, but Vinson had failed badly. When Warren assumed the position of chief justice, he knew that his skills as a manager would be tested as well as his understanding of the law.

# STATE THE TOPEKA JOURNAL

AN INDEPENDENT NEWSPAPER

By Stauffer Publications, Inc.

Topeka, Kansas, Monday, May 17, 1954 —Twenty-four Pages

Official City Paper

Home Ed

FIVE C

**FOLKS AND THINGS**

## By 2054 This Bill Should Be Terrific

By GORDON F. MARTIN
(State Journal Staff Writer)

LIKELY it was that Jim Lane and his Free State army raiders figured it weren't no crime to steal a hoss from a Kentuckian nohow.

However it was, some of Jim Lane's men couldn't be nothin' but a Southern sympathiser, and even if he had no slaves hisself, he couldn't be nothin' but a no-good Democrat who didn't deserve to own a hoss anyway.

So just go on out to his place southeast of town and git a hoss anytime you need one, boys. And don't bother to pay for it.

NOW MAYBE that's the way old Jim Lane used to counsel his Free Soil militia when "the boys" were ridin' around roughshod over anybody who got in their way. And maybe Lane's riders didn't have to be told about how to "git a hoss" without paying for the animal.

However it was, some of Jim Lane's men stole a couple of valuable horses from James B. Warren. They also took some guns, clothes and shoes, and some blankets too. James Warren itemized his losses when he filed a claim with the Shawnee county Probate judge against the Territory of Kansas.

Lane's men, he swore, took property with a value of $268.20, and took it at the point of a gun.

THAT WAS in 1856. Warren's claim was processed a year later but never paid.

Now nearly 100 years later, Warren's grandson, who is Frank J. Warren, former Topeka mayor, has earned compound interest which makes it worth $84,873.93 today.

A bill for that amount was presented to Governor Arn Monday by Warren who said, in a letter:

"The State of Kansas has owed the original amount of this claim for approximately 100 years and I feel sure my native state will want to make some arrangements to pay an honest debt that is long past due. In any event, I hope it will not be allowed to accumulate for my other Centennial, lest my grandchildren will have claim on all the state income and hazif the rial value."

WARREN said with a grin that he didn't expect to hold his breath until the state paid off. But he indicated that while the Centennial needs is a gag or two along with its historical aspect, and he says that he has had some enjoyable moments digging into family history in the state's Centennial year.

Warren's grandfather, James Warren, was a wagon boss on the old Santa Fe trail and after his bullwhacking days, he moved from his native Kentucky to a homestead on Deer creek. That was in 1854.

Frank Warren remembers how his father used to tell of Grandfather Warren's precautions against Free Soilers' raids on his farm home.

"Grandfather always had a horse saddled and ready," said Warren, "because they used to steal horses, or somethin'. I guess it was because he was a Kentuckian and a Democrat. His homestead was in the Deer creek area north of old Vinewood park."

THIS WAS Warren's letter to Governor Arn, outlining his Grandpa's claim, as shown by probate copies of records of the territorial probate court:

"I am enclosing herewith a claim as part of the estate of my grandfather, James H. Warren, in the amount of $84,873.93 for livestock, merchandise and equipment taken by force of arms ... Jim Lane and his Free State army during the month of September, 1856, approximately 100 years ago. This claim was properly processed and accepted by the state (Kansas Territory) on December 19, 1857.

"The claim at first glance may seem out of proportion to the original amount ($268.50). I figured the amount on the basis of compound interest which I believe is the only fair method that could be used in computing the amount due. I am not sure you are the proper official to burden with this just and unfortunate claim. While the original amount may not seem large, I am sure it was a tremendous loss to my grandparents who were working desperately to eke out a living on the plain they homesteaded on Deer creek 3½ miles southeast of Topeka on October

# SCHOOL SEGREGATION BANNE

## Turnpike Bonds Authorized So Suit Can Start

### Supreme Court Will Clear Legal Air in Friendly Action

The Kansas Turnpike authority Monday formally approved issuance of 140 million dollars in revenue bonds for the 234-mile proposed Kansas turnpike.

In so doing, the KTA deliberately stuck its neck out in a legal way to become a target of a friendly-type quo warranto suit by the state to determine the legality of the KTA's actions and the law under which it operates.

A quo warranto action in substance inquires of the defendant: By what right do you act in this master?

The state agency also incorporated in resolutions other actions and a set of bylaws thought necessary to offer Atty. Gen. Harold R. Fatzer something a challenge.

WILLIAM TIMMERMAN, assistant attorney general, said the suit would be filed within a few days.

The suit, to be filed as an original action in the Kansas Supreme court, is being brought to make sure no legal hitch develops after the turnpike gets under construction, and to facilitate the huge bond sale.

Altho the court has never ruled directly on any phase of the KTA, lawyers believe the high tribunal has ruled favorably on similar questions in other unrelated suits.

BESIDES AUTHORIZING the bond issue, the KTA named its Santa Fe headquarters for the turnpike, and specified regular meetings as the second and fourth Mondays of each month at 1 p.m. Special meetings can be called any time, with proper notice.

The KTA also approved entering a trust agreement with financial institutions to secure the bond issue, and receiving a proposal from the First Boston Corp. and Smith, Barney and Co., both of New York, Kansas municipal bond companies and as Kansas City, Mo., firms for sale of such bonds.

## Topeka Can Hear Centennial Star on Monday Night

Topekans will get a chance to preview the singing of Lucille Norman, feminine singing star of the Centennial pageant, Monday night.

Miss Norman will sing as a guest star in an original operetta "The Railroad Hour" at 7 p.m. McCarthy, claiming that "this cover up" made it impossible to get at the truth, declined to say, when asked by reporters, whether he might walk out on the hearings if the subcommittee acceded to Eisenhower's order.

THE PRESIDENT'S order was laid before the subcommittee when it convened, and received a calm reception at the time.

But later, Senator Jackson (D-Wash.), McClellan (D-Ark.) and Symington (D-Mo.) fired a few critical volleys at it.

McCarthy asked for a five-minute recess to confer with his aides, Roy M. Cohn and Francis P. Carr, about their course in the light of what he termed this "almost unbelievable situation."

RETURNING, he told the subcommittee: "I must admit I'm somewhat at a loss as to what to do at this moment."

"For some fantastically strange

State Journal Photo

### Laying Track at the Fairgrounds for 'Cyrus Holliday'

This special crew from the Santa Fe railroad was hard at work Monday morning putting down a 300-foot strip of track on which the 1880 Cyrus K. Holliday locomotive and one car will chug into the Centennial pageant. The operation was almost identical to the type of work done in early days to move the tracks across native prairie—rough-hewn ties, light rail and tracks laid directly to bare earth.

## Future of Probe Uncertain After President Rules

### Eisenhower Cloaks Top-Level Meeting on Army's Charges

**BULLETIN**

Washington, May 17 (AP)—Senators investigating the McCarthy-Army row Monday recessed until next Monday to give time to try to clarify a Presidential order forbidding further inquiry into high-level administration conferences.

Washington, May 17 (AP) —The future of the McCarthy-Army hearings was thrown in doubt Monday by a Presidential order—denounced by Senator McCarthy as an "iron curtain"— shutting off inquiry into whether "higher-ups" directed the Army's charges against the Senator.

The Senate investigations subcommittee recessed its public hearings at 11:55 am to consider in closed session what stand it might take on Eisenhower's order.

## Workmen Busy at Fairgrounds Setting Stage for Biggest Show

By BOB ROYER
(State Journal Staff Writer)

There was plenty of action at the Kansas Free fairgrounds Monday as workmen tackled the job of getting the area ready for the Centennial pageant.

Immediately in front of the grandstand, carpenters were rapidly putting up a 32x64-foot stage. Lighting equipment was rolling in from all directions.

Members of the Topeka stagehands union were installing the lighting equipment and moving scenery bracing out to the front of the grandstand.

To the last of the stage, a 15-man crew from the Santa Fe railroad were laying ties and rails for the Cyrus K. Holliday train.

AND THAT WAS a rather large operation in itself. The section gang doing the job was under the direction of John Laris of 705 Jefferson.

Trucks were moving second-hand ties into the area and dumping the mon the ground. Periodically a truck with several rails would drive up and dump off the

work for the specially-built stage in place. They, too, were hampered some by the mud of the dusk.

THE STAGE will be elevated 3 feet from ground level and have scaffolding and bracing at the rear for the scenery built by stagehands during the past few weeks.

William Meader, production director of the pageant, and Allen Cooke, his assistant, were sitting in the stands giving over last minute details on the stage and its construction.

Lighting equipment occupied a large area just to the west of the regular fairgrounds stage. Most of it is yet to be installed.

However, some of the heavy lighting equipment was already going up on decks attached to the grandstand.

## Buy Parade Seats Now, Committee Urges

Four thousand bleacher seats will be set up on the south side of the statehouse grounds along Tenth for Saturday's Centennial parade, but this number will be augmented if necessary.

Early demand has been brisk.

Ed Dyer, whose committee is carrying out this project, said an additional 3,800 seats will be brought from Kansas State college if demand warrants.

Those wanting parade bleacher seats are asked to buy them not later than Tuesday, at $1 apiece, at the municipal auditorium.

THEY POINTED OUT that bleachers have been put in hard seats just as was done in the early days.

"We're putting rails right across prairie and just like they used to do it," Urlacher said.

Tickets for the Centennial pageant at the fairgrounds May 22-28 are also on sale at the auditorium.

## Centennial Street Decorations Will Go Up on Tuesday

Decoration of downtown streets for Topeka's Centennial pageant at the fairgrounds May 22-28, will begin Tuesday.

The decorations which include red, white and blue banners, 6 by 11 feet, will be placed on electric light poles on Kansas from

### Supreme Court Refute Doctrine of Separate but Equal Education

### High Tribunal Fails to Specify When Practice of Dual Schools Must Be Dropped by States

Washington, May 17 (AP)—The Supreme court ruled unanimously Mond segregation of Negro and white students in public schools is unconstitutional it said it will hear further arguments this fall on how and when to end the p

Thus many months perhaps more time will elapse—before the historic ruling actually wipes out the separate schools now in existence in many states.

Chief Justice Warren read the court's opinion which declared:

"We conclude that in the field of public education the doctrine of separate but equal race has no place. Separate educational facilities are inherently unequal.

"THEREFORE, we hold that the plaintiffs (Negro parents and others similarly situated for whom the action has been brought are, by reason of the segregation complained of, deprived of the equal protection of the laws guaranteed by the fourteenth amendment.

"This disposition makes unnecessary and any discussion whether such segregation also violates the due process clause of the fourteenth amendment.

The fourteenth amendment was adopted after the Civil war, primarily for the benefit of slaves freed by President Lincoln. It says no state may deny any person due process and equal protection of the law, nor abridge their privileges of immunities.

THE CASES decided Monday —with the court's finding that segregation is unconstitutional —involved five states South Carolina, Virginia, Kansas, Delaware and the District of Columbia.

But lawyers said a ruling against segregation would affect a total of 17 states which have laws requiring separation of the races in schools, plus three other states having laws which permit —but do not require—segregation.

THE COURT was told the 17 states and the District of Columbia had 70 per cent of the nation's Negro population, or 10,322,496 Negroes out of a 15,-042,682 total. States with permissive segregation had an additional one per cent.

States whose laws require segregation had as follows: Delaware, Florida, Georgia, Kentucky, Louisiana, Maryland, Mississippi, Missouri, North Carolina, Oklahoma, South Carolina, Tennessee, Texas, Virginia and West Virginia.

States with permissive segregation were listed as New Mexico, Wyoming and Kansas.

AFTER reviewing a long line of decisions bearing on the "separate but equal" doctrine, Chief Justice Warren wrote:

"We come then to the question presented. Does segregation of children in public schools solely on the basis of race, even tho the physical facilities and other 'tangible' factors may be equal, deprive the children of the minority group of equal education opportunities? We believe that it does."

### Court Ruling Hailed

## Segregation Already En Here, Say School Officia

Jacob A. Dickinson, president of the Topeka I Education, hailed the Supreme court's segregatio Monday as "in the finest spirit of the law and mocracy.

"In my opinion, t has been very wise ciding the basic ques then calling for fur mission by all parti orderly and reasono plication of the Dickinson said.

THE TOPEKA Bo cation will, of course, the implementation o to terminate the maxi

For further details gation, see stories on s segregation in the e grades as rapidly as po

"The acceptance of by the people of Top country except for th former this decision of preme court with tem tion and genuine coo

SUPT. WENDELL said: "This action wil effect upon Topeka s cause segregation is being terminated in ii manner.

"During 1933-54 integrated. During 1954 trial Park, Clay, Crestvi Grant (partial), Oakla (partial), Potwin, Quin ton Heights, State St Sumner schools will grated.

"Subsequent steps taken in the light of a accumulated during the steps. I've not had t tunity to examine th ruling but I imagine t gation will be terminat pace before the Supre decides when and how he done?"

## Rainfall Spread Far Over State

### Oakley Is High With 2.08 Inches

More rain is predicted for the Topeka area Monday night after intermittent showers brought 60 inch to the city.

Beneficial rains fell Sunday over wide areas of Kansas, with northwest and eastern portions getting the most.

Oakley was high with 2.08. Other rainfall reports:

| | | | | |
|---|---|---|---|---|
| Chanute | .81 | Hiawatha | .40 |
| Coffeyville | .67 | Hill City | .52 |
| Concordia | 1.45 | Marion | |
| Dodge City | .53 | Ness City | .87 |
| Emporia | | Ottawa | .40 |
| Goodland | .43 | Pratt | .28 |
| Hays | | Wichita | .30 |

## Summary of Court's Segregation Ruling

Washington, May 17 (AP)— Here is the meat of the Supreme court's ruling Monday in the school segregation cases.

Segregation is unconstitutional—it violates the constitutional guarantee of equal protection of the laws.

A formal review ordering is stopped will be postponed until after arguments on special points are heard at the fall term.

Attorneys general of the states involved will be ordered to fill briefs by October 11 and to appear later before the court for further arguments on fixing an effective date when Negro students shall be admitted along with white children, and on how the order should be issued. This could be done either (1) by having a special master recommend specific terms for a final decree by the Supreme court or (2) by sending the cases back to lower federal courts for action.

Luncheon served at 11:30 am till 2 pm, Dining Room and Coffee Shop, Hotel Jayhawk AAA.—Adv

Rahn's Custom Tailoring $12 Kansas. —Adv

## The Forecast . . .

Forecast for Topeka and vicinity: Partly cloudy and mild Monday night with thunder showers tonight and Monday night Tuesday, partly cloudy, cooler Monday night. Low tonight 55.

For Kansas: Partly cloudy extreme northwest otherwise partly cloudy and mild Monday night with scattered thunder showers tonight and Monday afternoon or evening, spreading to east and central by night; Tuesday

## Day Before Big Celebration Starts

### Friday Night's Street Dan Will Climax Beard-Bonnet

# "EQUAL JUSTICE UNDER LAW": *BROWN V. BOARD OF EDUCATION*

The black community in Topeka, Kansas, was divided over the issue of school segregation. In the early 1940s, Lucinda Todd, an African-American former schoolteacher, was one of the first to challenge the inequalities among the schools. She wanted her daughter Nancy to learn to play the violin, but none of the black grade schools offered music lessons. When she saw a notice in the local newspaper announcing a concert by a grade-school orchestra representing what were said to be the 18 schools in the city, she took action. She began by telling the music supervisor that there were 22, not 18, grade schools in the community, then demanded to know why music instruction was not provided in the 4 schools that black children attended. The supervisor sent her to talk to the coordinator of black schools in Topeka. When the coordinator explained the absence of music from the curriculum by saying that black parents did not want music instruction and could not pay for instruments, she took her case to the board of education, and won.

Mamie Luella Williams, considered by many to be the best black teacher in Topeka, saw things differently than Lucinda Todd. She believed that the students who attended the all-black schools received at least as good an education as those who attended the all-white schools. She had good reason to hold this opinion: at two of the four black grade schools, more of the teachers held master's degrees than at any of the white grade schools, and their commitment to teaching was evident in their classrooms. When, in 1941, a lawsuit was brought by black parents to integrate the junior high schools, Williams shared her thoughts in a letter to the local black newspaper. Convinced that black teachers were more effective than whites in teaching black students, she wrote, "Those who are socially informed about people can help them best." Despite Williams's public defense of the city's all-black schools, the decision in this case of *Graham* v. *Board of Education of Topeka* ended segregation there, but only for a few years.

By 1950, school segregation was again the norm in Topeka, restored in part as a measure to protect the jobs of black teachers in the community. Oliver Brown, a former student of Mamie Williams, was not, however, content with the fact that his seven-year-old daughter Linda was having to commute a mile to the Monroe School when she could have walked to the all-white Sumner School a few blocks from their home. Just before the opening of the school year, Brown took his daughter to the Sumner School and attempted unsuccessfully to register her in the third-grade class. Linda waited outside the principal's office while her father went in. When he came out, she later recalled, he was "quite upset." Determined not to let the matter drop, Brown took his case to the local chapter of the National Association for the Advancement of Colored People (NAACP), which was actively seeking people to challenge the segregation in Topeka schools.

This case, combined with three other state cases and one from the District of Columbia, led to the Supreme Court's decision on May 17, 1954, declaring the doctrine of "separate but equal" to be unconstitutional. Using language that could easily be understood by the general public, Warren, the author of the Court's opinion, discussed the importance of education to society. Then he asked, "Does segregation of children in public schools solely on the basis of race, even though the physical facilities and other 'tangible' factors may be equal, deprive the children of the minority group of equal educational opportunities?" Without skipping a beat, he announced the Court's judgment: "We believe that it does."

Linda Brown, seated in the foreground, attended Monroe School, which provided African-American students with an education that was comparable to that of white students in Topeka. Her teacher, standing in the background, may have been more qualified than the white teachers at the Sumner School, located just a few blocks from Linda's home.

The impact of *Brown* v. *Board of Education* was enormous, establishing a precedent for a long line of cases involving racial discrimination relating to education, employment, public accommodations and services, and, above all, political participation. These decisions in turn led to federal legislation—the Civil Rights Act of 1964 and the Voting Rights Act of 1965—intended to guarantee "equal justice under law."

The decision was of great importance to the new chief justice as well. In his handling of this case, Warren established himself as a confident and capable leader, demonstrating good political instincts and strong management skills that quickly earned him the respect of his colleagues. These characteristics, along with his commanding presence, made possible the unanimous opinion that had eluded his predecessor but was considered essential if *Brown* were to be taken seriously.

Warren's opinion reflected his own values. He believed that education was a fundamental right, the means by which one could achieve individual success and contribute to the good of society as a whole. Well-educated voters, he argued, were essential to democratic government.

Warren also believed in equality of opportunity and respect for individual rights. During his 1948 Vice Presidential campaign, he had grown increasingly conscious of segregation and its effects on American society. Traveling through the South by train, he had been struck by the fact that blacks gathered on the opposite side of the railroad tracks from whites to listen as he delivered his campaign speeches.

When he returned to the campaign trail four years later, this time hoping to win the Presidential nomination, he endorsed several items important to blacks: a fair employment act, antilynching laws, and elimination of the poll tax, a fee imposed by many states to discourage African Americans—many of whom were desperately poor—from voting.

As chief justice, Warren was keenly interested in how laws affected people. Rather than relying solely on traditional legal reasoning—a method that involves extensive research of the law, analysis of precedents, reliance on established doctrine, and weighing of contradictory theories—Warren tended to reduce a case to a simple question of right and wrong or to raise the question, "What is fair?" While this approach has a certain appeal, it runs the risk of substituting a subjective "rule by men" for the more objective "rule of law," a concern that Warren's critics have consistently raised. In dealing with the issue of segregation, however, Warren could not help but ponder these moral questions and find the doctrine of "separate but equal" to be both unjust and unconstitutional.

The doctrine endorsing "separate but equal" facilities had been adopted by the Supreme Court in 1896. In *Plessy v. Ferguson,* the justices upheld a Louisiana law segregating black and white passengers on trains traveling within the state. The one dissenting vote was cast by John Marshall Harlan, a native of Kentucky and a former slave owner.

Harlan argued that segregation violated both the 13th and 14th Amendments, which had been adopted shortly after the Civil War. "We boast of the freedom enjoyed by our people above all other peoples," Harlan wrote. "But it is difficult to reconcile that boast with a state of the law which, practically, puts the brand of servitude and degradation upon a large class of our fellow-citizens, our equals before the law. The thin disguise of 'equal' accommodations for passengers in railroad coaches will not mislead any one, nor atone for the wrong this day done." The Court's official endorsement of the "separate but equal" doctrine in the *Plessy* case encouraged segregation by law and by custom.

By the end of the 19th century, many states had devised ways to prevent blacks from voting, such as literacy tests and poll taxes. They also adopted "grandfather clauses," which exempted men from meeting established voting requirements if their grandfathers had voted in the election of 1867—few black men had voted in that election. As a result, blacks rarely held government office. Because the white politicians who were elected tended to spend more tax dollars on facilities and services for whites, those provided to blacks were not only separate but almost always inferior.

In the 1940s, the Legal Defense Fund (LDF), the branch of the NAACP that handled litigation, adopted a strategy of chipping away at the doctrine of "separate but equal." The objectives were to determine whether federal judges were ready to reconsider the *Plessy* ruling and, if so, to establish precedents that could be used to challenge segregation in public schools. Thurgood Marshall, the chief lawyer for the LDF, brought five suits to the Supreme Court challenging the "separate but equal" doctrine on the ground that state university programs provided for black residents were not comparable to those established for whites. In each of these cases, the Court acknowledged the inequalities and required the states to allow blacks to enter previously all-white educational institutions.

On the basis of these victories, Marshall prepared to launch an attack on segregation in the public schools. This was a risky strategy. He could not be sure that the justices were ready or willing to find public school segregation unconstitutional. The rulings in the university cases affected a relatively small number of graduate students, whereas a decision involving the public schools would affect millions of children and thousands of teachers and was likely to meet with enormous resistance. Such a decision would strike at two principles considered fundamental by white—especially southern—political leaders: first, that state and local governments should have complete control over public education and, second, that states should have the power to establish racial segregation within their communities. Despite these obstacles, Marshall decided the time had come to push ahead.

The facts of the five public school cases combined under the *Brown* designation differed in certain respects. The elementary school in Topeka, Kansas, that Linda Brown attended was comparable to the elementary schools attended by white children. However, the one-room school that Shirley Bulah went to in Hockessin, Delaware, lacked indoor plumbing and was in no way equal to the school provided for white students, which had four classrooms, an auditorium, a basketball court, bus service, and modern toilets. Similar disparities were evident in the schools of Clarendon Country, South Carolina; Prince Edward County, Virginia; and the District of Columbia. What the cases had in common was the practice of separating black and white students.

Rather than emphasizing the inequalities among the schools, the lawyers for *Brown* and its four companion cases asserted that state-mandated segregation rested on the racist assumption that blacks were inferior to whites. The practice of separating students, they argued in their briefs, had the damaging effect of instilling in black children a sense of inferiority that undermined their academic performance and individual achievement.

The Supreme Court scheduled oral argument for December 13, 1952. Chief Justice Vinson, who presided the first time the cases were heard, was reluctant to overturn *Plessy.* A native of Kentucky, he feared the response that such a decision would meet with in the South, where many whites regarded states' rights and segregation as sacred principles. Justices Clark and Reed, who came from Texas and Kentucky, were also concerned about the impact desegregation would have on the South.

Justices Frankfurter and Jackson had reservations as well. Both men wanted to find a way to end segregation, but they questioned whether the Supreme Court had the authority to override state laws and local statutes requiring separate schools. Although Frankfurter eventually concluded that the Court did have that power, he recognized that the South was unlikely to obey a 5-to-4 decision. Fearing that the Court's prestige would be irreparably damaged if it handed down a split decision, he proposed to postpone the ruling on *Brown,* and the Court scheduled a second round of oral arguments for the next term.

As a result of Vinson's death and Warren's appointment to chief justice, Warren presided when the case was reargued in October 1953. Perhaps because he was a newcomer to the Court, he did not take an active role in questioning counsel. The two principal adversaries were John W. Davis and Thurgood Marshall. Davis was an imposing figure. A distinguished corporate and constitutional lawyer, he had been the Democratic Presidential candidate in 1924, ambassador to Britain, and solicitor general of the United States. Having argued many cases before the Supreme Court, he entered the courtroom confident of his ability to persuade the justices to uphold precedent and respect states' rights. "No man," he proclaimed, "will treat with indifference the principle of race. It is the key to history." Marshall was slightly more than half the age of his opponent. For nearly 20 years he had argued in both state and federal courts against the injustices of racial discrimination. Though less polished than Davis, Marshall had courage and conviction. As Warren later recalled, "Marshall made no emotional appeal, and argued the legal issues in a rational manner as cold as steel."

The new chief justice postponed discussion of the case until December. This hiatus gave him time to think about the issues, consider the consequences, and determine a course of action. When the justices met on December 12, Warren rather than Black was at the helm, which would not have been the case in October.

Warren's opening remarks shaped the discussion that followed. Rather than dealing with the constitutional questions raised by the case, he focused on the moral issues. The "separate but equal" doctrine, he explained, rested on the premise that blacks were inferior to whites. Because he was unwilling to accept that premise, he was determined to rule against segregation in public education. He admitted that he was unsure how to carry out such a ruling, but he was willing to take whatever time was needed to reach a solution.

Breaking from normal procedure, which was to vote on a case after each justice had expressed his views, the chief suggested that the Court postpone that step until later in the term. His reasoning was that his colleagues would be more likely to discuss candidly all aspects of the case if they had not already committed themselves to one side or the other. Over the next few months, the justices came back to *Brown v. Board of Education* on numerous occasions, tackling its troubling questions and, in the process, working out crucial compromises.

*Thurgood Marshall, flanked by George E. C. Hayes and James Nabrit Jr., argued the case against school segregation in the states. Hayes and Nabrit argued the federal case.*

The most important of these compromises called for two separate judgments. Several of the justices were reluctant to rule against segregation, solely because they feared the social and political upheaval that might follow. As a result, the first *Brown* decision, announced in May 1954, dealt only with the principle of segregation and whether it was right or wrong. *Brown II,* decided a year later, explained how the process of desegregating public schools should be carried out. By distinguishing principle from process, the southern justices were prepared to conclude that the "separate but equal" doctrine violated the 14th Amendment guarantee of equal protection under the law.

Although the challenges presented by *Brown* and its companion cases did not go away, Warren's approach gradually won over even the most reluctant of his colleagues. "It will take all the wisdom of the Court to dispose of the matter with a minimum of emotion and strife. How we do it is important," he cautioned at a conference on December 12, 1953. "My instincts and feelings lead me to say that, in these cases, we should abolish the practice of segregation in the public schools—but in a tolerant way." The Supreme Court, he believed, should provide basic guidelines but leave the task of deciding how to end segregation to judges in the federal district courts, who would be sensitive to local situations.

The justices cast their preliminary votes at the end of February 1954. Reed still planned to dissent, and Jackson intended to write a concurring opinion to explain how his reasoning differed from that of the majority. Warren assigned himself the task of writing the opinion for the majority, a job he shared with his three law clerks.

Before beginning the process of writing, the chief justice outlined his key points in a memorandum that he sent to his colleagues in early May. The opinions, he asserted, should deal only with public education, and should make clear that "separate but equal" schools have no place in

American society. The principal reason for overturning *Plessy* should, he argued, be the increased importance of education in the 20th century rather than a belated recognition that segregation had always been wrong. He concluded, "The opinion[s] should be *short,* readable by the lay public, nonrhetorical, unemotional, and above all, not accusatory. No section of the country and no segment of the population," he believed, "can justly place full responsibility for segregation on others. They must assume a measure of that responsibility themselves."

Warren wrote two opinions: one for the four combined state cases and a separate one for the District of Columbia case. Because these decisions were expected to have profound consequences, he took extraordinary security measures. He arranged for copies to be hand delivered to each of the associate justices for their comments and kept the originals in the walk-in safe just outside his chambers.

The many months of deliberation paid off. The justices made a few suggestions but, on the whole, responded with praise. William O. Douglas observed, "I do not think I would change a single word in the memoranda you gave me this morning. The two draft opinions meet my idea exactly. You have done a beautiful job." And on May 15, Stanley Reed changed his vote, which made the Court's decision unanimous. "There were many considerations that pointed to a dissent," Reed later explained. "They did not add up to a balance against the Court's decision. The factors looking toward a fair treatment for Negroes are more important than the weight of history."

The justices agreed to announce the decision on Monday, May 17. Journalists working in the pressroom in the basement of the building, as Richard Kluger recalled in his book *Simple Justice,* had been told that it "looked like a quiet day." Because reporters usually receive copies of the opinions from the court's press officer, they were surprised when he told them, "Reading of the segregation decisions is about to begin in the courtroom. You will get the opinions up there." Bounding up the long flight of marble stairs, they arrived as Warren began reading the *Brown* decision just before one o'clock. "These cases come to us from the States of Kansas, South Carolina, Virginia, and Delaware...."

Following the strategy that he had mapped out earlier, Warren declared, "We cannot turn the clock back to 1868 when the [14th] Amendment was adopted, or even to 1896 when *Plessy* v. *Ferguson* was written. We must consider public education in the light of its full development and its present place in American life throughout the Nation. Only in this way can it be determined if segregation in public schools deprives these plaintiffs of the equal protection of the laws."

The Court's unanimous opinion relied on sociological and psychological evidence to arrive at its conclusion that "separate educational facilities are inherently unequal." Warren asserted that "to separate [children] from others of similar age and qualifications solely because of their race generates a feeling of inferiority as to their status in the community that may affect their hearts and minds in a way unlikely ever to be undone."

Looking back to that historic moment, Warren remembered a "tenseness" in the courtroom when the decision was announced. "When the word 'unanimously' was spoken," he recalled, "a wave of emotion swept the room; no words or intentional movement, yet a distinct emotional manifestation that defies description."

Warren's colleagues readily acknowledged his role. Frankfurter dashed off a short note the day the decision was announced. *"This* is a day that will live in glory," he wrote. "It is also a great day in the history of the Court, and not in the least for the course of deliberation which brought about the result. I congratulate you." Harold H. Burton, too, was proud of the Court's achievement and recognized Warren's contribution to it. "To you goes the credit for the character of the opinions which produced the all important unanimity,"

The President and Mrs. Eisenhower
request the pleasure of the company of
The Chief Justice and Mrs. Warren
at a reception to be held at
The White House
Tuesday evening, December the first
nineteen hundred and fifty-three
at nine o'clock

*The Warrens' social life included frequent visits to the White House. However, cordial relations between President Eisenhower and Chief Justice Warren came to an end when, during a White House dinner party, the President tried to influence Warren's position regarding the constitutionality of school segregation.*

he wrote in a note to the chief justice on May 17.

Amid all the praise one voice was noticeably absent. President Eisenhower had supported, apparently with some degree of reluctance, Attorney General Brownell's decision for the Justice Department to participate in the case and to argue against segregation. However, once the case was decided, he made no public comment on the decision. His silence conveyed his displeasure not only with the ruling—he did not want the responsibility of enforcing a decision that he knew would meet with tremendous resistance—but also with Warren, his appointee. While the case was pending, Eisenhower had invited Warren to dine at the White House and had made quite clear his personal inclination to side with the South on the issue of segregation. Warren resented the President's meddling but did not respond. After the decision was announced, relations between the two men deteriorated rapidly and remained rocky throughout Eisenhower's administration.

The justices condemned the President's silence. Tom Clark later commented, "If Mr. Eisenhower had come through it could have changed things a lot." William O. Douglas was more forthright. "[I]f he had gone to the nation on television and radio telling the people to obey the law and fall into line, the cause of desegregation would have been accelerated. . . . Ike's ominous silence on our 1954 decision," he maintained, "gave courage to racists who decided to resist the decision."

The Court began work on *Brown II* as soon as the 1953–54 term came to a close. Warren requested ideas on how to proceed with desegregation and established a committee of six law clerks "to gather all information that might be of legal or practical value in meeting the varying conditions in the states where public school segregation is a problem." The committee's report served as the basis for judicial discussion and the Court's final ruling.

Warren initially planned to schedule oral argument after the November elections. Because of Associate Justice Robert Jackson's death in October, the hearing was postponed until March 1955 when the Senate confirmed the nomination of John Marshall Harlan II, grandson of the justice who had dissented in *Plessy*. The chief wanted to have a full court to deal with the difficult task of deciding how to end segregation in public schools.

Lawyers for the U.S. government and six southern states appeared before the Supreme Court in April. The justices allocated 14 hours—compared to the 1 hour normally allowed for oral argument—over a period of 4 days. The federal government called for an "immediate and substantial start" toward integration but urged the Court to delegate responsibility for its oversight to the local district courts. S. Emory Rogers, who had replaced John W. Davis as counsel for South Carolina, made it clear that his state had no intention of complying with *Brown,* regardless of what guidelines were established or which court exercised jurisdiction. At the end of an angry exchange with the chief justice, Rogers shouted, "I would have to tell you that right now we would not conform; we would not send our white children to Negro schools."

With good reason, the justices approached *Brown II* with caution. They did not want to issue an order that the southern states would refuse to obey. With that in mind, the chief urged his associates to take as much time as they needed before choosing a course of action. Once they agreed on the crucial points, recognizing that unanimity was as important to this ruling as it had been in *Brown I,* Warren began writing.

*Brown II* said as little as possible. Acknowledging the differences in local situations, the Court assigned district court judges the job of reviewing local plans for desegregation and overseeing the implementation of those plans. Where progress was slow, school boards would be held accountable, but judges were expected to be reasonable and to weigh fairly the efforts of local officials.

A few days before the Court announced its decision, Frankfurter told Warren, "I have now read this twice and I am ready to sign on the dotted line." He added, "I have only one further and minor remark to make." Referring to the timetable that school districts would be required to follow implementing the Court's decision, he explained, "I still think that 'with all deliberate speed'... is preferable to 'at the earliest practicable date.'" Three days later he again pressed his case. "I think it highly desirable to educate public opinion—the parties themselves and the general public—to an understanding that we are at the beginning of a process of enforcement and not concluding it." Reluctantly, Warren changed the wording.

Going along with Frankfurter proved to be a mistake. From a constitutional standpoint, it made no sense to declare segregation wrong but to allow it to continue until local and state governments became willing to accept the Court's ruling. As Thurgood Marshall observed, "I don't believe any argument has been made to this Court to postpone the enforcement of a constitutional right. The argument is never made, until Negroes are involved."

Frankfurter feared that the Court's reputation would be irreparably damaged if its decision in *Brown* were simply ignored. He was convinced that the South would be more likely to comply with the ruling if given time to get used to the idea of integrated schools and develop plans for gradual desegregation. Local southern officials saw things differently. They relied on the phrase "with all deliberate speed" to justify inaction; "deliberate," they were quick to point out, means "unhurried and methodical."

the standards certainly of those who at the start are, in the phrase of George

Orwell, "more equal". Integration could lower the standards of those now

under discrimination. It would indeed make a mockery of the Constitutional

process in vindicating a claim to equal treatment to achieve "integrated" but

lower educational standards. in en-

forcing the Fourteenth Amendment the Court is, broadly speaking, promoting

a process of social betterment and not of social deterioration. Court

fallible and finite, cannot in a day change a deplorable situation into the

ideal. It does its duty if it gets effectively under way the righting of a

wrong when the wrong is a rooted does its duty if

it that reverse the direction of the

So far as fashioning a decree is concerned, the problem before the

Court is a fact-finding problem. Only on the basis of facts not now

known will it be possible to judge how ills inherent in segregation of Negro

children can be terminated without substantially diminishing the

education for all children. The Court does not know that a simple

scrambling of the two school systems may not work. It is entitled to suspect

that this is so, it is surely entitled to suspect that spreading the

adjustment over time may be more beneficial to the total situation. When the

facts are found - no matter by whom - there are bound to be differences of

opinion concerning the judgment to be based on them. This is almost certain,

and hence future litigation is almost certain. The Court should take fore-

thought in restricting so far as may be both the area and the occasions for

such litigations.

5.      Plainly, therefore, an initial decree is bound to confine itself to

general terms, that the inequality of benefits which any segregated

school system begets for Negro children

the requirement that school systems be not disrupted

*This page from Associate Justice Frankfurter's memo to Warren regarding Brown II includes Frankfurter's handwritten corrections. In the middle of the page Frankfurter wrote the pivotal phrase "with all deliberate speed," which proved to be a loophole in the Court's decision that southern leaders exploited to stall desegregation efforts.*

Frankfurter's formula for gradualism became the justification for open resistance. Southern states with large African-American populations resisted the most strongly. They provided tuition for white students to attend segregated private schools, withheld funds from desegregated public schools, and, in some instances, closed schools that were integrated. Louisiana and Mississippi passed laws making attendance at a desegregated school a crime.

*In February 1950, Senator Joseph McCarthy of Wisconsin declared that he had a list of communists employed by the State Department. Neither Secretary of State John Foster Dulles nor President Eisenhower dared to challenge McCarthy's accusations. Eventually, however, the Senate conducted two months of hearings that pitted the U.S. Army against the senator and resulted in the Senate's censuring McCarthy by a vote of 67 to 22.*

# "Red Monday"

In the 1950s, fear of communism dominated American politics. The threat of communist expansion shaped foreign policy, and fear of subversion—the attempt to overthrow the government by individuals who supported the ideas and objectives set forth by the Communist Party—pervaded American life, including government policies and practices. The tendency of government officials to disregard individuals' basic constitutional rights as they carried out overzealous executive and legislative investigations of political dissenters resulted in dozens of lawsuits. Several of these made their way to the Supreme Court.

The economic troubles of the 1930s led thousands of blue-collar workers to blame the political and economic system for their unemployment, poverty, and despair. Many joined unions and participated in strikes in an effort to improve the plight of working people. The United Auto Workers, whose strikes against the major automobile makers in Detroit gained national attention, came to be viewed by business leaders, politicians, and journalists as communist sympathizers.

Troubled by the outbreaks of violence that often accompanied labor protests and by threats to international peace posed by Adolf Hitler and Benito Mussolini, in 1938 the House of Representatives established the House Un-American Activities Committee, or HUAC, and appointed Martin Dies, a Republican from Texas, as chair. "I am not in a position to say whether we can legislate effectively in reference to this matter [loyalty]," Dies confessed, "but I do know that exposure in a democracy of subversive activities is the most effective weapon that we have in our possession." "Exposure" in this context meant public accusation.

By the end of World War II, Americans saw the Soviets as their main enemy. With the coming of the cold war, HUAC directed its attention toward suspected communist sympathizers in the federal government. The Senate created its own investigating committee, the Internal Security Subcommittee. The Republican senator from Wisconsin Joseph McCarthy, who became chair of the committee in 1950, launched an aggressive campaign to identify, discredit, and punish Americans who had even remote connections to the Communist Party.

Under McCarthy's leadership, the committee disregarded procedures normally used to safeguard individuals' rights. Witnesses questioned by the committee were denied the right to a lawyer, were not told the charges brought against them, and were not allowed to cross-examine those who testified against them. Ignoring the fundamental legal principle that an individual is to be considered innocent until proven guilty, committee members began with the assumption that witnesses had to prove their innocence. They assumed that individuals were guilty if they relied on the 5th Amendment to avoid making statements that could be self-incriminating if taken out of context or intentionally distorted.

President Truman, responding to political pressures, ordered an investigation of all federal employees. By early 1951, the Civil Service Commission had determined that 3 million employees had no communist connections, but on

*text continues on page 92*

# McCarthyism and the Threat to Free Speech

*Warren shared his concerns about McCarthyism and its effects on free speech during a speaking tour of Midwestern universities in 1955. In a lecture given at Washington University in St. Louis entitled "The Blessings of Liberty," Warren focused on the responsibility of individuals—especially when elected officials seemed incapable of taking a stand—to defend their own basic rights and freedoms.*

I t is easier to know how to combat a foreign enemy who challenges our right to these freedoms and thus prevent a sudden collapse of the things we hold dear than it is to subject ourselves to daily analysis and discipline for the purpose of preventing the erosion that can with equal effectiveness destroy them.... Normally we can rely upon our representatives in government to keep our defenses sufficiently strong to enable us to ward off outside attack, but we cannot delegate to any or all of our government representatives the full responsibility for protection of our freedoms from the processes of erosion. Such protection can be had only through an understanding on the part of individual citizens of what these freedoms are, how they came into being and whether their spirit dominates our institutions and the life of our country....

Departures from the letter and spirit of our constitutional principles are not the product of any one person or any one group of persons. They are more properly chargeable to the entire body politic; to the suspicion, hatred, intolerance, and irresponsibility that stalk the world today; and also to a lack of appreciation of the age-old struggle of mankind to achieve our present blessings of liberty. Government—whether national, state, or local—is not the sole culprit in this matter. For it does not operate in a vacuum. In the last analysis it only reflects the mores, the attitudes, the state of mind of the dominant groups of society.

the basis of 14,000 full-scale investigations, the Federal Bureau of Investigation directed that 212 workers be fired. Another 2,000 employees resigned their government jobs, thereby avoiding federal probes into their personal and professional lives. During the Eisenhower administration, the federal government dismissed several thousand more employees.

In 1948, Congress had revived the 1940 Smith Act. Under that law, subversive activities became federal crimes, as did membership in organizations that favored the overthrow of the U.S. government. Twelve leaders of the U.S. Communist Party were arrested and charged under the Smith Act. The Supreme Court upheld their convictions in 1951. The key question was whether speech that called for overthrowing the government was alone sufficient for a conviction or whether evidence of subversive activities was also required.

Earl Warren had long harbored fears of communist subversion, which had influenced his decisions and policies while serving in elected office in California. As Alameda County district attorney, for example, he had kept files on labor leaders and others whom he suspected of harboring communist sympathies. In the controversy over loyalty oaths, he had opposed singling out university employees but, for security reasons, proposed requiring such oaths for all state workers, including university faculty and staff.

Warren was nevertheless aware of the dangers posed by legislative investigations. As early as 1939 he expressed concerns about HUAC. The committee, he charged, "starts with preconceived notions and its investigators go out to find supporting evidence. They bring that kind of evidence to the committee and suppress the evidence which will not support their theses."

As chief justice, Warren had more freedom to speak out against the investigations than did elected officials. Politicians depended on votes to keep their jobs, and according to a 1954 Gallup survey 70 percent of the American public approved of McCarthy and his tactics. Supreme Court justices, in contrast, are appointed for life. The founding fathers had created an independent judiciary specifically to ensure that its decisions would not be influenced by political pressures, and Warren used this independence to speak out against the dangers posed by executive and legislative investigations.

A variety of factors shaped Warren's response to McCarthyism, the most important of which was the lesson he had learned from Japanese internment during World War II. Under his leadership, the Court emphasized the need to respect "due process of law," in other words, to abide by the constitutional provisions for a fair trial. Several justices believed that this rule should be applied to federal investigations and Senate hearings as well, even though they were not technically trials.

In the 1950s, the Supreme Court had a number of opportunities to decide on cases involving national security. One that attracted a great deal of public attention was that of *Slochower* v. *Board of Regents of New York City,* the case of a German professor who lost his teaching position at Brooklyn University because he invoked the 5th Amendment when testifying before the Internal Security Subcommittee of the U.S. Senate. When asked if he had been a Communist Party member in 1940 and 1941, he exercised his constitutional privilege against self-incrimination. Under a New York City law that provided for the dismissal of employees who used the 5th Amendment to avoid answering questions relating to official conduct, he forfeited his job for refusing to answer. The Supreme Court found by a 5-to-4 vote that the city's law was unconstitutional on the grounds that it violated due process and made a mockery of the 5th Amendment's privilege against self-incrimination.

Another case that caught the public eye was *Jencks* v. *United States.* Clinton Jencks, president of a union in New Mexico, was charged with filing a false affidavit (a written statement made under oath) denying that he had any communist connections. He was convicted on largely circumstantial evidence provided by two informers paid by the FBI. One informer later confessed to lying. When Jencks's lawyers tried to gain permission to see the original reports submitted by the informers along with the later confession of perjury, the lower court denied permission. The Supreme Court, reviewing the lower court's decision, ruled that Jencks should be allowed to see reports submitted to the FBI by its paid informers. This practice was a logical extension of the 6th Amendment's guarantee of an accused criminal's right to be confronted with the witnesses against him and fell under the broad constitutional provisions requiring due process.

Under Warren, the Court challenged the policies and procedures that government officials were adopting to counter perceived threats to national security. These decisions produced rumblings of dissatisfaction among those who remained convinced of a communist threat. These reactions were minor when compared to the thunder of criticism that followed the Court's announcement on June 17, 1957—a day critics quickly dubbed "Red Monday"—of four decisions that reversed lower-court convictions of disloyalty.

The chief justice wrote the majority opinions for two of these cases, *Watkins* v. *United States* and *Sweezy* v. *New Hampshire.* Watkins, a labor organizer for the United Auto Workers, had been called to testify before HUAC. He had answered questions about his own earlier involvement with the Communist Party and that of others who were still members, but he refused to respond to questions about individuals who might have been communists in the past but were no longer. Such inquiries, he maintained, went beyond the limits of congressional authority.

Charged and convicted of contempt of court, Watkins petitioned, or asked, the Supreme Court to issue a *writ of certiorari,* an order calling for a lower court to send the legal documents relating to a case to the justices. A person petitioning the Court presents the question of law that is under dispute, citing the laws that the petitioner—the loser in the lower court—believes give the Supreme Court the authority to consider the case. The justices examine these petitions and, if at least four of the nine believe the lower court's decision should be reviewed, the Court grants the "cert."

The justices agreed to hear Watkins's case. They scheduled oral argument for March 7, 1957, and took up the case in conference on the following day. Warren led off: "The Committee must show why its questions are relevant." Echoing his 1939 statement about HUAC, he added that the committee does not "have the right to expose for the purpose of exposure." With the exception of Tom Clark, the other justices agreed. Because the decision would deal with actions taken by the House of Representatives and might thus be perceived as violating the separation of powers, Warren concluded that as chief justice he should be the one to write for the majority.

Warren adopted a cautious approach. Concerned that the Court might be accused of interfering with congressional affairs, he shifted some responsibility to the House of Representatives. Congress's power to conduct investigations, he wrote, is broad, but "it is not unlimited." Implying that the legislators had violated the constitutional principle of separation of powers, he declared that Congress is not "a law enforcement or trial agency. These are functions of the executive and judicial departments of government." He explained that Congress can not conduct an investigation without having a clear purpose, one directly connected to powers assigned to the legislative branch by the Constitution. Investigations motivated by a desire for publicity or intended to harm individuals are, he wrote, "indefensible."

*Sweezy* v. *New Hampshire* resulted from a state investigation of Dr. Paul Sweezy, who had given a guest lecture on the theory of socialism to a humanities class at the University of New Hampshire. Acting on powers granted him by the state legislature, State Attorney General Louis C. Wyman held hearings to determine Sweezy's loyalty. For the most part, Sweezy was cooperative. He answered questions about his past conduct and associations, denying that he had ever been a member of the Communist Party. He discussed his military service—he had worked in the Office of Strategic Services, the predecessor of the Central Intelligence Agency—and his role in organizing a Scientific and Cultural Conference on World Peace held in 1949.

Sweezy declined, however, to respond to questions not directly related to the issue of his loyalty. He refused to discuss political activities in which his wife and others had engaged or the content of the lecture. Wyman appealed to the Superior Court of New Hampshire, which found Sweezy in contempt and sent him to prison. The New Hampshire Supreme Court upheld the ruling.

Writing for the majority, Warren noted the similarities between this case and *Watkins* but also brought out the differences. In *Sweezy,* as in *Watkins,* the Court found that the legislature had not exercised adequate control over the investigations in that the legislators had not defined how or why their power could be used. As a result, the attorney general had inquired into the smallest details of Sweezy's past life, "thereby making his private life a matter of public interest."

"Our form of government," Warren declared, "is built on the premise that every citizen shall have the right to engage in political expression and association. This right was enshrined in the 1st Amendment of the Bill of Rights." Thinking, perhaps, of the influence that politicians such as Hiram Johnson had on his own thinking, Warren continued, "All political ideas cannot and should not be channeled into the programs of our two major parties. History has amply proved the virtue of political activity by minority, dissident groups, who innumerable times have been in the vanguard of democratic thought and whose programs were ultimately accepted. Mere unorthodoxy or dissent from the prevailing mores is not to be condemned. The absence of such voices would be symptom of grave illness in our society."

*Students at the University of New Hampshire enthusiastically endorsed academic freedom in the articles and editorials that appeared in the campus newspaper soon after charges were brought against Paul Sweezy. University President Robert F. Chandler Jr. issued a carefully worded statement in which he described the university as "a place where all political questions can be analyzed, studied, and discussed without particular feeling."*

The fact that the New Hampshire investigation had threatened academic freedom as well as more general rights of speech and association raised particular concerns for the Court. "No one should underestimate the vital role in a democracy that is played by those who guide and train our youth," Warren wrote. "To impose any strait jacket upon the intellectual leaders in our colleges and universities would imperil the future of our nation.... Scholarship cannot flourish in an atmosphere of suspicion and distrust. Teachers and students must always remain free to inquire, to study and to evaluate, to gain new maturity and understanding; otherwise, our civilization will stagnate and die."

Warren did not write the opinions in the other two cases decided on June 17, "Red Monday." However, he voted with the majority in *Yates* v. *United States* and joined a unanimous Court in *Service* v. *Dulles.* In *Yates,* the Supreme Court overturned convictions of Communist Party leaders who had been charged under the Smith Act with conspiring to overthrow the U.S. government. In this opinion the justices distinguished between a statement of ideas and speech intended to result in action. In *Service,* the Court determined that John Service, a State Department officer, should be given his job back, because the inquiries regarding his loyalty had not produced sufficient evidence to justify his dismissal.

Reactions to these decisions were mixed. A *New York Times* editorial entitled "A Day of Freedom," observed that "the shameful tactics of a number of Congressional committees in the past clearly come within the scope of the Chief Justice's comments. With this admirable opinion *[Watkins]* on the record, supported by six of the seven participating justices, it will be considerably more difficult for aspiring demagogues to pursue such tactics in the future." In contrast, a Virginia newspaper, the *Richmond News Leader,* accused the justices of "flagrant and willful disregard of the judicial function," and the *New York Daily Mirror* asserted that the Court had made "Communists superior to every other citizen in the country."

Privately, Eisenhower was furious with the decisions; publicly, he asked Americans to respect the Supreme Court and described it as "one of the great stabilizing influences of this country." The Georgia legislature passed a resolution calling for the impeachment of the chief justice, and the United States Congress came within one vote of passing legislation that would reverse these Supreme Court rulings.

The most serious reaction took place among the justices on the Court. In response to this public criticism, two of the justices—Felix Frankfurter and John Marshall Harlan— began to retreat from the Court's position, despite the objections of Warren, Black, Brennan, and Douglas.

Philosophical and personal differences contributed to rocky relations among the justices. The friction between Frankfurter and other members of the Court resulted from the bossy way in which Frankfurter treated others. Frankfurter, who was known as "the professor," wrote long memos that instructed his colleagues what they should think and how they should act. His lectures at the weekly conferences— which, as one of the justices observed, were always 50 minutes long, precisely as long as his classes at Harvard Law School—

seemed insulting to the intelligent, thoughtful, and conscientious men he was addressing.

Warren got along well with Tom Clark, John Marshall Harlan, and Stanley Reed—all of whom had very different views from his. Yet Warren's closest friends among the associate justices were those who, like the chief, believed the Court should take an active role in protecting the rights of individuals and upholding the principle of "equal justice under law." By 1955, Warren had identified Black as an ally and regularly stopped by his office to talk over cases, strategies, and opinions. When he retired, Warren spoke with affection and respect for the senior associate justice. "Having Hugo Black at my side for sixteen years," Warren said, was "one of the great privileges I enjoyed on the Supreme Court." He also got along well with William O. Douglas, a crusty outdoorsman from Washington State.

Warren formed his closest friendship with William J. Brennan. Both men were sons of immigrants who were active in labor unions. Brennan had excelled as a student— first at the University of Pennsylvania, then at Harvard Law School, where he had been a student of Frankfurter. He served in the New Jersey courts for three years as a trial court judge before moving up to the state supreme court. He was an advocate for the rights of the accused and an outspoken critic of McCarthy.

Brennan's thinking ran parallel to that of Warren. They had similar views regarding the role of the judiciary and shared liberal opinions on most constitutional issues. As a result, the two men worked together closely for more than a dozen years. Brennan's superior legal skills strengthened Warren's arguments, which were founded in practical and ethical reasoning. For some of the most important cases, the chief assigned opinions to Brennan, knowing that the results would capture his own views in convincing legal language. In dealing with the thorny issue of obscenity, this was the strategy Warren adopted.

# An Executive Apology

*President Eisenhower's displeasure with the Supreme Court's "Red Monday" decisions found its way into print when a newspaper reporter overheard a private conversation and saw an opportunity to make headlines. Eisenhower's carefully worded apology to Warren does not dispute the President's unhappiness with the Court's rulings.*

June 21, 1957

Dear Mr. Chief Justice:

As I have told you, I rarely read beyond the headlines on the front page of my newspaper. However, this morning I was told that some enterprising reporter has a story that at a private party I severely criticized the Supreme Court, expressing anger. I have no doubt that in private conversation someone did hear me express amazement about one decision, but I have never even hinted at a feeling such as anger. To do so would imply not only that I knew the law but questioned motives. Neither of these things is true.

So while resolving that even in private conversations I shall be more careful of my language, I do want you to know that if any such story appeared, it was distortion.

With warm regard,

As ever,
D.E.

*In his reply, Warren follows Eisenhower's lead, shifting responsibility to the press in order to avoid sharp disagreement over the issues themselves. His strategy is to reaffirm the Court's practice of not reacting to press reports, regardless of their content, but of allowing decisions to rise or fall on their own merits.*

*The case of* Wilson v. Girard, *to which Warren refers, involved an American soldier who had accidentally killed a Japanese woman during firing practice on a base in Japan. The question raised was whether to try the soldier in a Japanese or a U.S. court.*

*At the meeting of the American Bar Association in London, which Warren refers to in the closing paragraph, the attending lawyers accepted "without debate and without protest" a report condemning the Supreme Court's decisions in* Watkins, Sweezy, Yates, *and* Service. *As a result, Warren resigned from the organization.*

July 15, 1957

Dear Mr. President:

Your letter of June 21st, concerning the gossip column, arrived just as I was leaving for the Pacific Coast to spend a few days with my children. Realizing that they would still be writing similar things at the time of my return, I postponed answering it until now.

It was considerate of you to write, but it was in no sense necessary. Those of us who have long been in the public service know that some columns are written in ignorance and others to deceive. Whatever the reason, if unfounded, they should be ignored.

So far as some of the articles about our recent opinions are concerned, the writers could not possibly have read them unless there was a deliberate purpose on their part to deceive. While in other positions, I could and did speak out to counteract such statements. Here we do not respond regardless of what is said. We must live with what we write and are contented to do so. Some of the things which were written about the Court are as silly as those they have written about the purpose of your civil rights bill and your action in the Girard case. I am sure the only thing for us to do in such instances is to tune out on them and trust the future to vindicate both our actions and intentions.

Nina and I are leaving Wednesday for London with the American Bar Association, and we are looking forward to a pleasant visit. I hope that you and Mrs. Eisenhower will have a refreshing vacation at your new summer home.

Sincerely,
Earl Warren

# 8

# IS ALL SPEECH "FREE"?

Despite his demanding workload as chief justice, Earl Warren found ways to maintain a balance between his professional responsibilities and personal interests. During the week, he focused on his job, maintaining a disciplined schedule in order to complete his work. But by Saturday afternoon he was ready for a change of pace. He had always loved sports and frequently watched games on the weekends, live or televised. Professional sports appealed to Warren and his "old-fashioned" sensibilities.

In many respects, Warren embodied the attitudes and values conveyed in the famous Norman Rockwell illustrations then appearing on the covers of the *Saturday Evening Post*. A contemporary of Warren's, Rockwell admitted that he consciously, "paint[ed] life as I would like it to be." His drawings of American life—family outings and holiday gatherings; friendly policemen and returning soldiers; boyish pranks and youthful innocence; baseball, football, and scouting—communicated the ideals that the chief justice openly embraced.

By the standards of her times, Nina Warren was the ideal wife and mother. While the Warrens were living in

California, she had devoted nearly all her time and energy to home and family. In Washington, D.C., her responsibilities changed because their oldest children had married and were starting families of their own, and the youngest were attending college in California. As the wife of the chief justice, Nina Warren accompanied her husband to state dinners, diplomatic receptions, and other ceremonial affairs.

Every fall, Warren reserved a railroad car to transport the justices and their wives to Philadelphia for the Army–Navy football game. Potter Stewart, Harold H. Burton's replacement, turned out to be a Washington Redskins fan. Byron R. ("Whizzer") White, who was appointed in 1962, had played professional football for the Pittsburgh Pirates (the team was renamed the Steelers in 1940) before practicing law. Both men accompanied the chief to local games.

Warren was no doubt relieved to discover that most of his colleagues shared his interest in sports. Baseball was particularly popular. When Warren took the newly appointed William Brennan on a tour of the court building in the fall of 1956, the final stop was a lounge on the third floor. The

*Warren, along with Yogi Berra and Mickey Mantle, attended the ground-breaking for Toots Shor's new restaurant in New York City in October 1960. Warren loved baseball and enjoyed talking about the game as much as he enjoyed watching it.*

room was dark when they entered. The other justices were huddled around a black-and-white television in the far corner watching the World Series between the New York Yankees and the Brooklyn Dodgers. Warren switched on the light and attempted to make introductions, but the other associates were more interested in watching the game than in meeting their new colleague and protested the interruption.

Clerks who served under Warren have told of messengers delivering updates on World Series play to the justices, both in conference and during oral argument. Warren himself attended at least one World Series game each year he was on the Court. A fan of the Washington Senators, he went to as many of their home games as he could manage.

As was true of most of the justices, Warren developed close relationships with the men who clerked for him. On Saturdays he often took them to one of the clubs in town for lunch. Mealtime conversations, often lasting two or three hours, covered a wide range of topics, including the work of the Court, world events, and Warren's political career. As one former clerk recalled, "He would talk about simple principles, about what government should do—the whole package of middle-American, 1940s idealism sort of stuff. That's what he believed, right down to the core of who he was."

Warren's own values dictated the advice he gave his clerks. He attempted to steer them away from private law practice toward teaching or public service. When Dallin Oaks, his clerk for the 1957 term, was considering private practice in Chicago, the chief counseled against it. Oaks, who kept a journal during his year as Warren's clerk, recorded his boss's advice. "Chicago," according to the chief justice, "was a terrible place to live due to the crookedness of the government (including judiciary), the hoodlumism and racketeering which [were] prevalent, and the generally low moral tone." A few years later Warren approved of Oaks's decision to take a teaching position, explaining, "You'll be able to influence young lawyers. That's a wonderful thing to do."

Despite their geographic separation, Warren's family remained important to him. Virginia and Dorothy moved to Washington, D.C., but the other children were still on the West Coast. Twice a year, the Warrens returned home to California to visit family and friends. Warren usually spent his summer vacations hunting and fishing, activities he had shared with his sons when they were growing up. During the winter holidays, the Warrens visited their children and grandchildren. They regularly attended the Rose Bowl parade—for which Warren was the grand marshal in 1955—and the Rose Bowl game in Pasadena later that day.

To a great extent, Earl Warren was able to transform Norman Rockwell's ideals into reality in his own private life. That was not the case, however, when it came to shaping public attitudes and values. He was deeply troubled by the changing mores of society. What he viewed as declining moral standards seemed to him to threaten not only the social fabric—the integrity of the individual and the stability of the family—but also the political system, the very success

*Warren served as grand marshal of the Rose Bowl parade in 1955. Despite rainy weather, the chief justice and his wife carried out their official duties with great poise and watched Ohio State defeat Southern California, 20–7, on the muddy field of the Rose Bowl.*

of democratic government. In one series of cases involving the publication and distribution of obscene materials, Warren attempted to impose his own values on the larger society while upholding freedom of speech and freedom of the press, which are guaranteed by the 1st Amendment.

In dealing with obscenity, the Court asked whether government could limit the distribution of books, films, magazines, or other publications. Justices Black and Douglas maintained that the 1st Amendment prohibited all forms of censorship, regardless of content. The remaining justices, including Warren, disagreed. They argued that obscene publications were not protected from government restrictions.

The problem was that neither Warren nor any of his associates was prepared to define obscenity. Warren refused to watch films that had been labeled as obscene, relying instead on Brennan's judgment or that of his clerks, and he dismissed print publications that were labeled indecent as "garbage." Potter Stewart remarked simply, "I know it [obscenity] when I see it." Furthermore, the justices were unwilling to serve as a national board of censorship or to delegate to others the responsibility for judging materials. With the possible exception of Warren, the justices recognized the difficulty of separating their personal attitudes and values from established legal and constitutional principles and feared that any effort to classify materials would undermine their reputation as impartial judges. Warren tended to see moral and constitutional issues as being inseparable.

*Roth* v. *United States,* decided on June 24, 1957, resulted from a federal statute passed in 1873 known as the Comstock Act. Originally intended to prohibit the mailing of information about birth control and abortion, the Comstock Act was later used to prevent the distribution of obscene literature. The U.S. District Court had convicted Samuel Roth of violating the law on the ground that he had sent obscene pamphlets and advertisements through the mail. Roth appealed, asserting that the Comstock Act was unconstitutional. The

Circuit Court of Appeals upheld his conviction, and the Supreme Court heard the case in April 1957.

At the conference to discuss *Roth,* Warren indicated that he would uphold the conviction, maintaining that "the federal government must have a right to protect itself." In other words, the government must have the authority to pass and enforce legislation aimed at immoral actions that could destroy the foundations of democratic society.

Justice Brennan, the author of the majority opinion, concluded that "the unconditional phrasing of the First Amendment was not intended to protect every utterance." He argued that "all ideas having even the slightest redeeming social importance—unorthodox ideas, controversial ideas, even ideas hateful to the prevailing climate of opinion—have the full protection of the guaranties." But, he observed, "implicit in the history of the First Amendment is the rejection of obscenity as utterly without redeeming social importance," noting that it is "not within the area of constitutionally protected speech or press."

In a concurring opinion, Warren took a different tack. On the one hand, he wished to preserve the 1st Amendment's protections for free expression. He was concerned that government censorship might come to extend to "great art or literature, scientific treatises, or works exciting social controversy." On the other hand, he believed strongly that the distribution of obscene materials—at least those he himself would classify as obscene—should be prohibited.

In order to reconcile these positions, Warren attempted to distinguish between the person distributing the materials and the obscene publications themselves. "It is not the book that is on trial," he wrote, "it is a person. The conduct of the defendant is the central issue, not the obscenity of a book or picture." In drawing this distinction, he believed the Court could rule against the criminal actions of the defendant and avoid the problem of judging the materials themselves and thus limiting the scope of the 1st Amendment.

Warren's reasoning was faulty. In order to conclude that Samuel Roth had broken the law, it was necessary to examine the materials in question to determine if they were obscene. Whether he was willing to admit it or not, the freedoms of speech and press were absolutely central to this case.

In the case of *Kingsley Books* v. *Brown,* decided the same day as *Roth,* the Court upheld a New York law that allowed the state to exercise "prior restraint," to determine whether publications were obscene in order to prevent their distribution. In this ruling the chief justice dissented, because the law empowered the police to act and the courts to rule before publishers had sold their materials. Using the same faulty logic he had relied on in *Roth,* he maintained that "this New York law places the book on trial. . . . It is the conduct of the individual that should be judged, not the quality of the art or literature. To do otherwise is to impose a prior restraint and hence to violate the Constitution."

In the 1961 case *Times Film Corporation* v. *Chicago,* the justices dealt with movies, a form of communication for which no clear precedents existed. Consequently, they needed to determine whether movies were protected by the 1st Amendment and, if so, whether that amendment prohibited censorship in every instance. Chicago had established a licensing board to review all movies before they were shown in public theaters. Times Film applied for a license to show *Don Juan,* a movie based on Mozart's opera *Don Giovanni,* but the company refused to submit a copy of the film to the reviewers, intentionally challenging the city's power to censor speech. Although the movie was not obscene by any standard, the board denied the license because it had not seen the film. Times Film then charged that the licensing requirement violated the 1st Amendment. The Supreme Court did not agree. In a 5-to-4 decision, Justice Clark held that the 1st Amendment does not protect against prior restraint in all cases and indicated that motion pictures were not necessarily governed by the same rules as other forms of expression. Each form of communication, he observed, "tends to present its own peculiar problems."

Warren, joined by Black, Douglas, and Brennan, dissented. Expanding on arguments used in the two earlier cases, he insisted that government should presume that individuals will use the freedom of expression in morally and socially responsible ways; it should presume innocence and not permit censorship. "The First Amendment," he argued, "was designed to enlarge, not to limit, freedom in literature and in the arts as well as in politics, economics, law, and other fields.... Its aim was to unlock all ideas for argument, debate, and dissemination. No more potent force in defeat of that freedom could be designed than censorship."

Warren's authoritative tone here was misleading. His defense of the freedom of expression sounded uncompromising and strong, yet he continued to believe that local communities could set standards that would allow them to maintain a "decent" society. In *Jacobellis* v. *Ohio,* a 1964 case in which Warren voted to uphold the conviction of a theater owner who had shown an obscene film, he stated, "There must be a rule of reason in this as in other areas of the law."

Shortly after retiring from the Court, Warren described the challenges he and his colleagues had faced in dealing with obscenity cases. Pornography, the chief claimed, was the Court's "most difficult area [because] we have to balance two constitutional rights with each other." Government has a "right to a decent society"—a right, it should be pointed out, that is not specifically stated in the Constitution—yet as the 1st Amendment clearly states, "Congress shall make no law... abridging the freedom of speech, or of the press." Warren explained that his goal had been to reestablish "a moral tone for our nation [that would] restore public and private language to generally accepted norms of decency." In this, he admitted, the Court had failed completely.

*On Wednesday, November 20, 1963, President and Mrs. Kennedy hosted a reception for the Supreme Court justices and their wives. The Kennedy administration and the Warren Court shared strong commitments to civil rights, church-state separation, and opportunities for education.*

# 9

# INVESTIGATING JOHN F. KENNEDY'S ASSASSINATION

Cold, clear weather, with temperatures hovering around zero, failed to discourage thousands of well-wishers who crowded around the Capitol building on January 20, 1961, for the inauguration of President John F. Kennedy. Bracing himself against the biting cold, the newly elected Massachusetts Democrat called upon his "fellow Americans" to "ask not what your country can do for you" but to "ask what you can do for your country." As chief justice of the United States, Earl Warren administered the oath of office and, with his wife Nina, remained in the reviewing stand with the new President until the last band had marched by at six P.M. Kennedy, in a note of thanks, expressed appreciation "for the generous role" Warren had "played in the Inauguration ceremonies" and for his "cheerful endurance."

Although he was a Republican, Warren had voted for Kennedy, primarily because he felt compelled to vote against Richard M. Nixon. He simply did not trust Nixon. Yet, at the time of the 1960 election, Warren also had serious concerns about the Democratic candidate. John F. Kennedy had served in the U.S. Senate, but he had not been in office long enough to establish a strong record that one could use to judge his abilities as a leader. He remained in a certain sense an unknown quantity.

Warren's initial doubts about the new President soon dissolved. Unlike Eisenhower, Kennedy directed his attention to problems involving social justice. His younger brother, Senator Edward Kennedy, recalled that, "the Executive worked in tandem with the judiciary, taking strong initiatives in civil rights, and laying the groundwork for an upheaval in criminal and civil justice by focusing on the problems, ventilating them [drawing public attention to them], and proposing administrative and legislative reforms. By the end of the first decade of the Warren Court," he observed, "Congress also began to complete what the Court had started." Warren and his colleagues welcomed these opportunities for cooperation.

JFK also extended his personal friendship to the chief justice. Shortly after taking office, Kennedy made an unscheduled appearance at a birthday celebration arranged for Warren by his former clerks. Two years later, the President sent Warren a note expressing appreciation "for the dignity and wisdom of your judicial leadership in the past ten years. Although it is not possible for all of us to be your clerks," he wrote, "in a very real sense we are all your students."

On November 20, 1963, the White House held a reception for the Supreme Court justices and their wives. Warren, obviously on good terms with his host, joked about the President's upcoming trip to Dallas. "Watch out for those Texans," he remarked. "They are a wild bunch."

Two days later, a messenger interrupted the Court's weekly conference with news that Kennedy had been shot. Justice William O. Douglas later recalled that historic moment: "The old Chief read the message to us and then broke down and wept, tears running down his cheeks." "The Chief's attitude toward JFK," Douglas explained, "could be called fatherly. He thought the world of the man and spoke very frequently of him in affectionate terms."

*text continues on page 114*

# PUBLIC RECOGNITION

*The University of California School of Law in Berkeley marked Warren's 10th anniversary as chief justice by naming the new wing of Boalt Hall the Earl Warren Legal Center. The chief attended the groundbreaking ceremonies there on September 27, 1963, as did seven of his colleagues from the Court. Just days before the groundbreaking, President Kennedy wrote conveying the admiration he felt for Warren.*

THE WHITE HOUSE

WASHINGTON

September 23, 1963

Dear Mr. Chief Justice:

I hope that you will permit me to make this brief out-of-court intrusion into the ceremonies which are being held this week by your brethren of the Court and by the Bar in recognition of the full decade you have served as Chief Justice.

You have presided over the work of the Supreme Court during ten years of extraordinary difficulty and accomplishment. There have been few decades in our history when the Court calendar has been crowded with so many issues of historic significance. As Chief Justice, you have borne your duties and responsibilities with unusual integrity, fairness, good humor, and courage. At all times your sense of judicial obligation has been unimpaired by criticism or personal attack. During my time as President, I have found our association to be particularly satisfying, and I am personally delighted that during this week you will receive not only the acclaim of Californians, but also the respect and affection of all Americans whose common destiny you have so faithfully helped to shape throughout your public career.

Sincerely,

The meeting came to an abrupt halt. The justices retreated to their chambers where, shocked by the event, they spent the next couple of hours huddled next to their radios, listening to broadcasts from Dallas and wondering who was responsible, why such an act of violence had been committed, and what effects the crime would have on the country. They were struggling with these unanswered questions when news of the President's death reverberated across the nation. Later that evening, a dutiful chief justice awaited the arrival of Mrs. Kennedy on the President's official airplane, Air Force One, at Andrews Air Force Base near Washington. Lyndon B. Johnson, already sworn in as President, accompanied Kennedy's widow on the flight home.

Jacqueline Kennedy called Warren on Saturday, November 23, and asked him to speak at a memorial ceremony scheduled for Sunday afternoon in the Capitol rotunda. As he was finishing his speech that morning, his daughter rushed into the office to announce that Lee Harvey Oswald, the principal suspect in the assassination, had been shot and killed while in police custody. Warren was stunned.

At JFK's memorial service the chief justice was one of three speakers. Mike Mansfield, the Senate majority leader, and John W. McCormack, the speaker of the house, preceded the chief justice. Deeply troubled by the hatred and

*Chief Justice and Nina Warren, at the White House, mourn the death of John F. Kennedy. Jacqueline Kennedy asked Warren to deliver a eulogy at the President's memorial service held on November 24, 1963, in the Capitol rotunda.*

violence that were plaguing American society in the early 1960s, Warren allowed his thoughts and feelings to find expression on this solemn occasion. "What moved some misguided wretch to do this horrible deed may never be known to us," he conceded, "but we do know that such acts are commonly stimulated by forces of hatred and malevolence such as today are eating their way into the bloodstream of American life. What a price we pay for this fanaticism!"

Desperately grasping for something good to come out of this tragedy, Warren continued, "If we really love this country; if we truly love justice and mercy; if we fervently want to make this Nation better for those who are to follow us, we can at least abjure the hatred that consumes people, the false accusations that divide us and the bitterness that begets violence. Is it too much to hope that the martyrdom of our beloved President might even soften the hearts of those who would themselves recoil from assassination, but who do not shrink from spreading the venom which kindles the thoughts of it in others?"

One week after the assassination, President Johnson sent Deputy Attorney General Nicholas Katzenbach and Solicitor General Archibald Cox to meet with the chief justice. They informed him of Johnson's plan to establish a commission to investigate Kennedy's assassination and of the President's desire to appoint Warren chairman. Because the justices had an agreement that the members of the Court would not accept outside appointments, Warren immediately declined.

Later that day, the President invited Warren to the White House, where Johnson pressed his case. Already rumors were circulating, raising questions about the assassination that would normally have been settled in a trial. Because Oswald had been murdered, there would be no trial. Johnson had decided that the best way to address the fears of the American people would be to establish a commission to examine the evidence, draw conclusions, and issue a report. In addition to asking Warren to chair this commission, the President intended to appoint a half dozen leaders from both parties: senators Richard B. Russell (Georgia) and John Sherman Cooper (Kentucky), congressmen Hale Boggs (Louisiana) and Gerald R. Ford (Michigan), former CIA director Allen W. Dulles, and former assistant secretary of the navy and Presidential advisor John J. McCloy.

Warren remained reluctant to take on the assignment. In addition to his many judicial responsibilities, he believed that his serving on a Presidential commission would violate the constitutional principle of separation of powers. Johnson, well known for his powers of persuasion, appealed to Warren's patriotic sensibilities. "You were a soldier in World War I," he reminded the justice, "but there was nothing you could do in that uniform comparable to what you can do for your country in this hour of trouble." Rumors of international conspiracy, he hinted, could lead to war. Faced with such dire predictions, Warren agreed to serve.

On November 29, 1963, Johnson issued an executive order formally establishing the President's Commission upon the Assassination of President John F. Kennedy, and Congress granted it broad powers to carry out the investigation. The commission held its first meeting on December 15, 1963, at which time, Warren recalled, the members "assessed our task and agreed that we...were merely a factfinding body." Although the commission's hearings were held in private, every witness was allowed to have a lawyer present and to request that the examination be conducted in public. The American Bar Association sent an observer, whose job was to make sure that the hearings were carried out with due respect for individuals' rights.

The commission chose J. Lee Rankin, a former solicitor general, to serve as chief counsel. Rankin had 14 assistants, of whom half were experienced lawyers who offered advice and the others recent graduates from leading law schools, who did most of the work. The commission decided to rely on reports from the Federal Bureau of Investigation and the Central Intelligence Agency. Its members assumed—incorrectly, as it was later revealed—that these two federal agencies would openly and honestly share the information they were collecting related to the assassination. At the beginning of February 1964 the commission began gathering information independently. Its members questioned 94 witnesses and collected testimony from 552 witnesses with knowledge pertaining to the crime.

During the investigation, Warren, usually with the support of Rankin, made a number of controversial policy decisions. One involved the mentioned reliance on FBI and CIA reports. The commission's members began to doubt they were receiving complete and accurate information. However, because at the time of the investigation neither the press nor politicians had begun to investigate the practices of these two federal agencies, Warren decided not to challenge the reports they submitted. Looking back, this was probably a mistake. Critics and skeptics today regularly cite flawed information that came from the FBI and the CIA when challenging the conclusions drawn by the Warren Commission.

Even more unpopular was Warren's decision not to circulate, even to the commission members, photographs of Kennedy after the shooting and X rays taken as part of the autopsy. Several factors may have influenced him in this decision, the most important of which was respect for the Kennedy family. Years later, Rankin explained that Robert Kennedy had requested that "the x-rays...not become part of the official record of the Commission." These materials, Kennedy insisted, were too private, and Warren agreed. Because Warren intended to make public all the evidence used by the commission, he refused to allow other members to examine the photographs and X rays. When they asked if these materials would assist in drawing critical conclusions, Warren called in a physician, who explained that they merely confirmed the coroner's report, which the members had already examined.

Because President Johnson's purpose in establishing the commission had been to settle once and for all the questions relating to Kennedy's assassination, Warren reasoned that the report resulting from the investigation had to be unanimous. To achieve that goal, he took charge of rewriting sections of the final report in order to satisfy all the commission members. The main point of contention was whether Oswald had acted on his own. The evidence pointed in that direction, but Richard Russell maintained that they could not be absolutely certain. Therefore, he objected to any assertion that rejected pointblank even the remote possibility of a conspiracy. Warren's carefully crafted statement therefore explained that the commission had "found no evidence that either Lee Harvey Oswald or Jack Ruby [the man who killed Oswald] was part of any conspiracy, domestic or foreign, to assassinate President Kennedy."

*On September 24, 1964, Warren delivered the report of the special commission appointed to investigate the assassination of President Kennedy. Attending the formal presentation were, from left to right, McCloy, Rankin, Russell, Ford, Warren, Johnson, Dulles, Cooper, and Boggs.*

The final report, including the evidence used by the commission, was published in the fall of 1964. The initial response was positive. Johnson, who left office in 1968, never wavered in his appreciation for Warren's labors. "Chief," he later remarked, "of all the things you have done for your country, the most important was your work with the Commission on the Assassination of President Kennedy."

Warren himself described the assignment as "the unhappiest time of my life.... [T]o review the terrible happenings of that assassination every day [was] a traumatic experience." Yet he defended the work of the commission and the report it produced. "If I were still a district attorney and the Oswald case came into my jurisdiction, given the same evidence, I could have gotten a conviction in two days and never heard about the case again." He insisted, "No one has produced any facts that are contrary to the Commission's conclusions."

Lingering uncertainties nevertheless led the House of Representatives to conduct its own investigation of Kennedy's assassination in 1978. House members questioned whether Warren and his colleagues had covered up certain facts in order to arrive at a simple, preconceived conclusion—that a single gunman had been solely responsible for the crime. The House Select Subcommittee on Assassinations, which reviewed the work of the Warren Commission and issued a report in December 1978, found that "the investigation into the possibility of conspiracy in the assassination was inadequate," a deficiency that it said was "attributable in part to the failure of the Commission to receive all the relevant information that was in the possession of other agencies and departments of the Government." An audiotape released toward the end of the subcommittee's investigation pointed to a high probability that shots had been fired from two locations, suggesting the possibility of a conspiracy. The subcommittee's members, aware that Warren and his colleagues had not had access to this and other evidence, asserted, "The conclusions of the investigation were arrived at in good faith, but presented in a fashion that was too definitive."

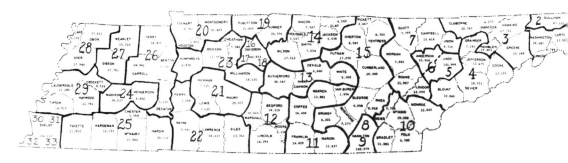

Apportionment of the Tennessee Senate set out in Senate Bill No. 5 (as amended) of the First Extraordinary Session of the 82nd General Assembly

Adopted by the Senate, June 4, 1962
Adopted by the House, June 6, 1962
Signed by the Governor, June 7, 1962; became Chapter No. 3

Smallest figures represent population 21 years of age or older in each county, according to the 1960 Federal Census

TENNESSEE SENATORIAL DISTRICTS - 1972

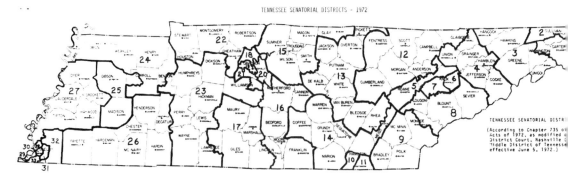

*The Supreme Court's decisions establishing the principle of "one man, one vote" for both branches of the state legislatures required states to reconfigure their electoral districts. For example, in Tennessee, the urban area of Memphis in Shelby County (the county in the lower left corner of the state) had one representative in 1962, indicated by the number 32 on the map. In 1972, after the Court mandated reapportionment, Memphis was broken into several small districts, giving the heavily populated urban area four representatives in the state Senate.*

# 10

# ONE MAN, ONE VOTE

In 1961 the Supreme Court agreed to hear a lawsuit brought by a group of Tennessee voters who claimed that a state statute passed in 1901 denied them equal representation under the law. The statute established districts for election to the state's two legislative assemblies. By law, representatives were chosen from each district by registered voters. Despite a requirement in the Tennessee constitution that districts were to be adjusted as the population changed, the state legislature had not reapportioned the state's electoral units for more than 60 years. In the meantime, the balance of the population had moved from rural to urban areas. Because the boundaries remained as they were when drawn at the beginning of the century, the rural districts had relatively few voters, while the urban units had many—in some cases 19 times the number of voters in rural areas. Yet the rural districts and their urban counterparts both had the same number of representatives in the state legislature.

Similar inequities existed in 40 of the 50 states. In Vermont, for example, one member of the state legislature represented 49 people; another represented 33,000. After the 1950 census, the 15,000 residents in the three northern counties of California had the same representation in the state senate as the 7 million people who lived in Los Angeles County.

When Los Angeles petitioned for reapportionment in 1948, then-governor Warren was an outspoken opponent of the idea. As governor, he had benefited politically from the existing system, and he was not alone. Throughout the country, elected officials were reluctant to adjust the electoral districts in their areas for fear of losing their jobs. Consequently, political power remained largely in the hands of a minority of voters who lived in rural areas. The chief justice later admitted, "I was just wrong as Governor." He told one of his clerks, "As a political matter it seemed to me to be a sensible arrangement. But now, as a constitutional matter, with...the responsibilities of a Justice, I...look at it differently."

To a great extent, Warren's judicial outlook was shaped by his faith in the democratic process. For democracy to work, he believed, each voter had to have an equal voice in the political process. The Constitution, he knew, originally gave the states the authority to set their own requirements for voting and holding office. After the Civil War, however, Congress and the states approved amendments to the Constitution that limited states' power. The 14th Amendment dictates that no state can "deny to any person within its jurisdiction the equal protection of the laws," and the 15th Amendment declares that "the right of citizens...to vote shall not be denied or abridged...on account of race, color, or previous condition of servitude." More than 50 years later, the 19th amendment gave women the vote. These changes represented a determined effort to make the U.S. government more democratic. Warren concluded that the amendments provided the necessary tools for the Court to use in repairing the political system.

Until 1960 the justices had refused to deal with the inequalities widely recognized to exist in electoral districts, although they had been given many opportunities to do so.

In that year, during the height of the civil rights movement, the Court decided that the electoral districts in Tuskegee, Alabama, violated the 15th Amendment because they undermined the influence of black voters. The lines for city council election had been drawn so that only five black voters remained within the city limits. For purposes of municipal elections, the other 400 blacks were no longer classified as voters.

The Tennessee case of *Baker* v. *Carr* did not deal with racial discrimination. In this case, Charles W. Baker, chairman of Shelby County Quarterly Court, sued Tennessee's secretary of state Joseph Cordell Carr for the purpose of securing financial benefits for the city of Memphis. Warren knew that by reducing the political influence of urban residents, state legislatures had been able to ignore the needs of minorities and low-income workers, a large percentage of the urban population. He also recognized that the equal-protection clause in the 14th Amendment did not apply solely to African Americans. What was not clear was whether the equal-protection provision guaranteed the right to have an equal say in the political process.

Before appealing to the Supreme Court, the plaintiffs—the parties who had brought the suit—had asked the state courts and the federal district court to rule on the case. But the judges in all these courts had refused, explaining that judges did not have the power to resolve controversies involving the political process. The principal question raised in the Tennessee case was whether the judiciary had the authority to force a state legislature to change its electoral districts, to make them equal in terms of population. When the justices first discussed the case, they were divided, with no group holding a clear majority. Warren therefore had to rely on his management skills to lead the Court to one of its most important decisions during his tenure as chief.

Justices Frankfurter and Harlan were convinced that the Court did not have the power to act on this issue. Reapportionment, they maintained, was a political question, which the Court had no authority even to consider. Justice Charles E. Whittaker refused to commit himself. Appointed to the Court by President Eisenhower in 1957, Whittaker lacked the outstanding credentials of his colleagues and, as a result, often shied away from making controversial decisions. Given that the justices disagreed on whether the Court should deal with the issue of reapportionment, he concluded that they should take no action.

Warren agreed with the plaintiffs that the imbalance among electoral districts in the case under consideration was "a violation of equal protection" guaranteed by the 14th Amendment. He was certain that the Court should act. However, he did not think that in this case the Court should do more than declare that it had the authority to deal with the issue of legislative apportionment.

Potter Stewart, who had convinced the Court to postpone a decision for several months because he could not make up his mind, eventually concluded that the inequalities among districts were so great as to require judicial action. Though he was willing to exercise judicial power, he wanted more evidence that the legislators had in fact intended to give certain voters a larger voice than others before ordering changes in the Tennessee political system.

In contrast, Justices Black, Brennan, and Douglas were convinced that the districts in Tennessee needed to be reapportioned. They believed the Court should declare its power to act *and* order changes. Justice Clark, who initially had not wanted the Court to intervene, changed his mind and sided with his three liberal colleagues. When Clark realized that the plaintiff, Baker, did not have any other way to achieve his goal of electoral equality, he concluded that it was not enough for the Court to declare that it could act if it so chose. The Court, he believed, should require reapportionment in Tennessee. As a result of ongoing discussions among the justices, Warren shifted his position and decided the Court should require redistricting. This created a majority but left Stewart on his own, agreeing on the more important point of requiring action but unwilling to go beyond that.

The chief therefore had to make a strategic decision. If the majority decided to assert the Court's authority and require Tennessee to reapportion its districts, they would lose Stewart. The vote would then be only 5-to-4, on an issue of tremendous significance. In order to keep Stewart, the majority would have to limit its decision. In addition to counting the votes, Warren took into account that Stewart had supported judicial action several months before Clark had changed his vote. Warren wanted to be fair to Stewart, which in this case he believed meant limiting the Court's opinion so that Stewart could join with the majority.

The chief then had to decide who should write the opinion. He chose Brennan, because he was the only other justice willing to compromise. On March 26, 1962, the Court declared only that it had the power to compel reapportionment of the states' electoral districts.

Conservatives criticized the decision, claiming that the Court, composed of appointed—not elected—officials, had no right to meddle in the political process. Legislators, they argued, should set their own rules and, if they failed to make the needed adjustments, be voted out of office. Liberals recognized that the electoral system, as it had evolved, would not correct itself. Consequently, they applauded the Court's work. Attorney General Robert F. Kennedy called *Baker* v. *Carr* "a landmark in the development of representative government." President Kennedy also approved of it. "The right to fair representation and to have each vote count equally is," he stated, "basic to the successful operation of a democracy."

Within a year, voters brought lawsuits in 36 states calling for reapportionment of electoral districts. Cases from Alabama, Colorado, Delaware, Maryland, New York, and Virginia made their way to the Supreme Court. Warren chose the Alabama suit, *Reynolds* v. *Sims,* as the lead case and scheduled oral argument for late November 1963. The justices had

*Attorney General Robert F. Kennedy, a committed supporter of civil rights, visits the Morningside Community Center in Harlem in 1963. Urban voters, such as the future voters in this photograph, gained representatives under the Court's reapportionment decisions and with the increased legislative power were better able to advance the concerns of their communities in state government.*

just completed discussing the *Reynolds* case on November 22 when they learned of Kennedy's assassination.

Warren decided to write the *Reynolds* opinion himself. Justice Frankfurter had retired from the Court in 1962, leaving Harlan the sole dissenter in the reapportionment cases. The remaining justices agreed that the governing principle for selecting members of the lower house of the state legislatures should be "one man, one vote"—in other words, based on population. Initially, they had thought that, as in elections for the U.S. Senate, geography could serve as the basis for representation in the upper house of the state legislatures.

As the chief worked on this case, he began to realize that the comparison between the federal government and the states was incorrect. Each of the original 13 states was a sovereign state; in other words, each had been completely independent. In the process of joining together, the states formed a federation, which is why the United States is referred to as having a federal government. The same was not true for the geographic units within the states. Counties, for example, have never been independent political units; they are simply administrative divisions, carrying out the policies and enforcing the laws adopted by the state government.

This realization led Warren to conclude that the electoral districts for both the lower and upper houses of a state legislature should be based on population. Black, Brennan, and

Douglas immediately agreed with this reasoning. So did Arthur E. Goldberg, who had taken Frankfurter's seat on the Court. Byron White, who had succeeded Whittaker, eventually bought the argument as well.

Warren prepared a detailed outline of the opinion but turned the actual writing of it over to his clerk, Francis X. Beytagh. (The chief often delegated the writing of opinions to his clerks, overseeing their work and revising the final drafts.) Because he was also chairing the commission to investigate Kennedy's assassination during the 1963–64 term, Warren had become increasingly dependent on his clerks. Beytagh recalls Warren frequently calling him at home on weekends to discuss the *Reynolds* case. He also claims credit for the wording, now famous, that captures the essence of Warren's thinking: "Legislators represent people, not trees or acres. Legislators are elected by voters, not by farms or cities or economic interests."

On June 15, 1964, Warren announced the 8-to-1 decision of the Court requiring redistribution of the seats in both branches of the Alabama legislature. The public reactions were mixed. Anthony Lewis, a Supreme Court reporter for the *New York Times,* labeled June 15 as "one of the great days in the Supreme Court history." His colleague Arthur Krock by contrast worried that the public would get the impression that "the Constitution...provides for the correction of any social or political condition that the majority of the Court deems undesirable and endows the Court with the power to take the functions of another branch of government when that branch fails to act."

Conservative politicians were furious. Senate majority leader Everett Dirksen proposed a constitutional amendment that would allow voters to decide whether to implement the Court's reapportionment rulings. But the Senate defeated that measure—by just seven votes—allowing the Supreme Court's rulings to stand.

| DATE ARRESTED OR RECEIVED | CHARGE OR OFFENSE (If code citation is used it should be accompanied by charge) | DISPOSITION OR SENTENCE (List FINAL disposition only. If not now available submit later on FBI Form R-84 for completion of record) |
|---|---|---|
| 7-5-1963 MARICOPA COUNTY | COUNT I-KIDNAPPING COUNT II-RAPE(FIRST DEGREE) TO RUN CONCURRENTLY | 20 yrs. to 30 yrs. |

| OCCUPATION | RESIDENCE OF PERSON FINGERPRINTED | |
|---|---|---|
| TRUCK DRIVER | WIFE: TWILA MIRANDA 157 E. COMMONWELL CHANDLER, ARIZONA | |

If COLLECT wire reply or COLLECT telephone reply is desired, indicate here

☐ Wire reply   ☐ Telephone reply

..........................................
Telephone number

FOR INSTITUTIONS USE ONLY

Sentence expires ......... 7-5-1993

ARIZONA PRISON JULY 6 1963 24638

FD-249 (Rev 4-27-62)

*In 1960, Ernesto Miranda was picked up by the police in Arizona and charged, as this report indicates, with kidnapping and rape. Following their decision in* Escobedo v. Illinois, *the justices were eager to clarify the guidelines they had established regarding the right to legal counsel. The case brought by Miranda allowed them to answer a critical question: When does the right to counsel begin?*

# THE ROAD TO
# *MIRANDA*

Public reaction to the Warren Court's decisions was sharply divided, and strongly stated. The most controversial issues included the desegregation of public schools and accommodations, the defense of free speech and association, and the prohibition of school prayer, an issue the Court settled in two highly publicized decisions in the early 1960s. President Eisenhower, though disappointed by Warren's performance, attempted to convince the public that relations between the executive and judicial branches of government were friendly. In private, he confided that appointing Warren to the Court was "the biggest mistake" he had made since taking office.

Congressmen and senators alike responded to a number of the Court's actions with legislative proposals aimed at undoing the supposed wrongs committed by the Court. Conservatives, typically Republicans and southern Democrats, led the attacks on the Court. Their efforts were defeated by moderates and liberals. In 1958, for example, then Senate Majority Leader Lyndon B. Johnson used his influence to persuade Democratic party members to be "absent" or "unavoidably detained by official business" when a proposal to limit the Court's powers was to be voted on. The purpose of this strategy was to ensure defeat of a popular but constitutionally flawed bill without harming the reputations of those who opposed it. By a single vote, the Senate defeated the bill, which the House had approved 241 to 155.

In 1957, right-wing political groups began calling for Earl Warren's impeachment. The most visible of these organizations was the John Birch Society, led by candy manufacturer Robert Welch. With an annual budget of $8 million and a membership approaching 100,000, the society played on fears aroused by the cold war, claiming that the Supreme Court was undermining national security. In a January 1961 statement Welch charged that the Supreme Court was "now so strongly and almost completely under Communist influence that it shatters its own precedents and rips gaping holes in our Constitution in order to favor Communist purposes."

The chief justice dismissed the personal attacks with characteristic good humor, but viewed the attacks on the Court in quite a different light. He was deeply troubled by a proposal, endorsed by nearly two-thirds of the state legislatures, to create a Court of the Union, made up of chief justices from all 50 states, with the power to review and overturn Supreme Court decisions.

He was also disturbed by hostile reactions to rulings regarding the rights of accused criminals. Beginning in 1956, the Supreme Court made a number of decisions—reflecting Warren's own commitment to establishing rules governing criminal procedure—intended to extend the rights contained in the 5th, 6th, and 8th amendments to all individuals accused of criminal acts.

*In his office, Warren posted a* New Yorker *cartoon depicting Whistler's mother embroidering a pillow with the slogan "Impeach Earl Warren." He joked that the billboards plastered across the countryside "do make evident that we have freedom of speech in our country."*

The rulings in these cases resulted from the justices' conviction that democratic government requires "equal justice under law."

Of course, Warren was not alone in recognizing that the criminal justice system does not treat all defendants alike. However, because he had served as a district attorney for more than a dozen years, he was well acquainted with how law enforcement operated and was committed to correcting the inequalities caused by social and economic differences. His goal in these cases was to establish clear guidelines for putting into effect the rights guaranteed in the Constitution so that all Americans, not just the privileged few, would be protected from unfair practices.

In a series of moves that signaled a significant shift in criminal law, the Court found that rights protected by the federal constitution also applied to the states. Until this time, state constitutions had governed criminal prosecutions in cases involving state but not federal law. Because state constitutions did not include all the rights guaranteed by the federal constitution, accused criminals had thus far often been denied fundamental protections, including the right to avoid self-incrimination, the right to confront opposing witnesses, the right to a speedy trial, and protection against cruel and unusual punishment. Troubled not only by the differences among the states but also by discrepancies between state and federal standards, the Court acted to create a more uniform code of law.

As part of a far-reaching effort to guard the rights of those unable to pay for legal services, the justices decided that a convicted criminal who wants his or her case reviewed but cannot afford to pay for a copy of the transcript of the original trial must be given that document in order to carry out the appeal process. A few years later, they concluded that a defendant who wants to appeal a conviction is entitled to the help of a lawyer and that the state must pay the cost of counsel if the individual cannot. As Justice

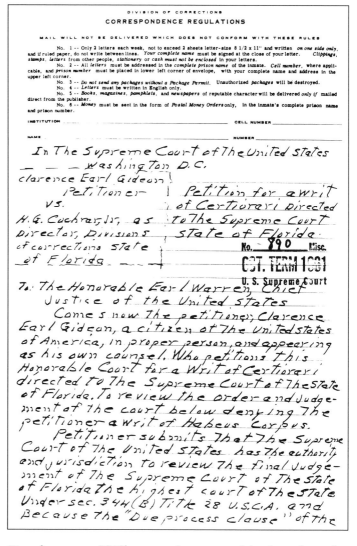

Douglas wrote, "[T]here can be no equal justice where the kind of appeal a man enjoys depends on the amount of money he has."

One of the most famous cases, *Gideon* v. *Wainwright* (1963), held that the right to counsel is "fundamental and essential to a fair trial" and, for that reason, must be honored in state as well as federal courts. Clarence Earl Gideon had been arrested for breaking and entering into a Florida poolroom. When he was brought to trial, the state judge refused to appoint a lawyer to defend him, even though he could not afford to hire one. Gideon attempted unsuccessfully to defend himself. While in prison, he prepared a handwritten petition to the Supreme Court, asserting that he had been denied "due process of law," guaranteed by the 14th Amendment, because he had not been represented by counsel.

Gideon assumed, incorrectly, that the Supreme Court had already granted this right. But in 1942 the Court had ruled otherwise, declaring that a state did not have to provide a lawyer unless the defendant was being tried for a capital crime—that is, one for which the punishment is death—or the defendant could show that there were "special circumstances" involved. This proved to be a vague guideline that meant different things to different judges.

Warren, dissatisfied with this precedent, had as a result instructed his clerks to look for a case that would allow the Court to reconsider the earlier decision. The *Gideon* case had all the right elements, and by a vote of 8-to-1 the Court agreed to review it. Warren appointed a brilliant lawyer, Abe Fortas, to defend Gideon. Fortas's oral argument, Justice Douglas later remarked, was the best he had ever heard, which came as no small praise from a justice who had then served for 36 years. In the end, the justices voted unanimously to overturn the 1942 ruling. Because Hugo Black had dissented from the earlier ruling, Warren assigned him the task of writing the opinion. The Court announced its decision on March 18, 1963.

The following year, the Court expanded the practical meaning of the right to counsel guaranteed by the 6th Amendment to include not only one's defense at a criminal trial but also representation during a police interrogation. In this case, Danny Escobedo, a murder suspect, had been denied the right to speak to his lawyer while being questioned by police, even though the lawyer was present in the police station and had requested to see his client. He eventually confessed to the crime. The Court, in a 5-to-4 decision, threw out the confession and held that the accused must be allowed to consult counsel once he or she becomes the prime suspect in a case.

*Escobedo* v. *Illinois* settled, by the closest of votes, the right of an accused criminal to consult an attorney during a police interrogation, but it did not answer the question of when the right to counsel begins. The Court needed to clarify its new rules, and that required another decision. Warren now asked his clerks to look for a case that would allow the Court to complete its work of laying out guidelines for police officers to follow. Warren's clerks found 150 cases that raised issues relating to police procedures. These cases came to the Court in a period of 18 months from 25 state courts as well as federal appellate courts. The justices considered 101 of these.

They chose four, including *Miranda* v. *Arizona.* In this case, the accused, Ernesto Miranda, had been arrested and taken to a police station in Phoenix for identification and questioning. After two hours of intense interrogation, with no lawyer present, Miranda finally confessed to committing two serious crimes, rape and kidnapping, and signed a written statement to that effect. This statement was used as evidence at the trial, and Miranda was convicted. His lawyer claimed that he had not signed the statement "voluntarily, knowingly, and intelligently" and that he had never been advised of his right to counsel. The police later admitted that they had informed Miranda neither of his right to talk to a lawyer before he was questioned nor of his right to have his attorney present during the interrogation.

During oral argument, Warren made it clear that, in his opinion, the right to counsel began as soon as an individual was arrested. He also pointed out the need to advise a defendant of his or her rights, suggesting that the accused could make a more intelligent decision if given all the relevant information. At the judicial conference the chief followed the same line of reasoning, adding that the FBI routinely "read" a defendant his or her rights at the outset of an interrogation. The fact that the FBI followed this procedure, Justice Brennan recalled, was "a swing factor... perhaps the critical factor in the *Miranda* vote."

Although Warren assigned himself the task of writing the majority opinion, the final product turned out to be a joint effort. The chief justice sketched out the main points of his argument in a handwritten outline that served as the basis for his initial draft. Then Brennan, demonstrating his skill as a legal technician, responded to the draft with a 21-page memo in which he attempted to clarify the language, organize the argument, and explain more fully the reasoning behind the decision. He also answered questions raised by earlier decisions involving the right to counsel as well as objections offered by the four dissenters in this case.

Black, too, offered suggestions, the most important of which urged the chief to delete specific charges against the southern states. Warren had cited reports that "Negro defendants were subjected to physical brutality—beatings, hanging, whipping—employed to exhort confessions." "The files of the Justice Department," he noted, "abound 'with evidence of illegal official action in southern states.'" In an internal Court memo, Black tactfully explained why these accusations should be omitted:

> When I read [these passages] it struck me that some of the Court's critics would immediately say that our holding is but another phase of the racial question, when of course that is not true at all. Also, your reference to the "Southern States"... would likely be over-emphasized by many as an indication that what we are doing is to attack the South. Your whole opinion absolutely refutes any such possible implication but nevertheless I would hope that you could shift the emphasis... so as to deprive all of the slightest basis for intimating any such criticism of your opinion.

*text continues on page 137*

# THE *MIRANDA* PRINCIPLES

*Before writing the opinion, Warren sketched out the principles he intended to discuss in* Miranda. *These points were based on specific constitutional provisions and also on his deeply rooted belief that individuals, regardless of their financial resources, should be equal before the law.*

D efendant's right to counsel unless he knowingly and intelligently waives it commences at least when he is taken into custody (under some circumstances before arrest). The police have no right to arrest a person or take him into custody against his will for the purpose of interrogation.... Under the constitution the criminal case against [the] defendant commences then. This does not mean that a lawyer must be appointed for him at that time. This need not be done until some further meaningful action is taken against him. One of the meaningful things the police cannot do is interrogate him unless he is adequately advised of his rights and legally waives them. He must be advised fully of [the] right to remain silent, etc. and of his right to counsel, that if he is indigent the court will appoint a lawyer for him.... He cannot be either threatened, cajoled or tricked into such a waiver. If this is done, the waiver is not effective. No distinction should be made between a defendant who already has a lawyer, ... and one who has none at the time, nor between one who can reach a lawyer at the time and [one] who for any reason cannot. Nor should any distinction be made between those who have the means to hire a lawyer and those who do not....

The above principles do not and should not retard the police from making any investigation of the defendant while he is in custody—that would not be lawful for them to make otherwise. These rules will not provide absolute protection of the weak, illiterate or poor defendant against the possibility [of] 5th amendment violations, but I believe it is the best we could do to give such people the same rights as the rich, the organized criminal and the knowledgeable who will always insist on their right to counsel.

Black also took issue with Warren's contention that the Court was enforcing the protections of the 5th Amendment against self-incrimination because forced confessions were "repellant to civilized standards of decency." He asserted that "we should enforce that protection because the Fifth Amendment requires it. . . . The test for me is the language of the Fifth Amendment, the one and only test."

Warren announced the *Miranda* decision on June 13, 1966. In addition to Black and Brennan, Douglas and Fortas (who had replaced Goldberg) made up the majority. The opinion, which was divided into three parts, began by describing the strategies and procedures used by police during interrogations. It explored the historical reasons behind the 5th Amendment's proscription of self-incrimination. In conclusion, it listed the four things that police officers must tell defendants before they begin to question them: They have the right to remain silent; anything they say can be used against them; they have the right to counsel; and if they cannot pay for counsel, lawyers will be provided for them.

These rules, now referred to as the *Miranda* warning, illustrate Warren's approach to the law. Not satisfied with merely voicing lofty ideals, he sought to find ways to turn constitutional principles into practical policies and workable programs that would benefit all Americans. Committed to fairness, equality, and justice, the principles of democratic government, he provided the means by which individuals are informed of and able to exercise their rights in the most critical circumstances.

# POLITICAL QUAGMIRES

Political events of the late 1960s convinced Earl Warren that it was time for him to retire from the Court. On March 31, 1968, Lyndon Johnson announced that he would not seek reelection to the Presidency. Outspoken criticism of his Vietnam War policies, declining health, and, above all, a poor showing in the early Presidential primaries convinced the Texas Democrat to leave politics. Robert F. Kennedy, determined to complete the work begun by his slain brother, confidently launched his own campaign to win the democratic nomination. Focusing attention on the enormous inequalities of opportunity among Americans, Kennedy established a strong following among party liberals. Had he lived to secure the nomination, he would have been a strong contender for the Presidency in the November elections.

Robert Kennedy's assassination on June 5, 1968, just minutes after he acknowledged victory in the California primary, had profound, long-term consequences for the nation. Kennedy, Warren believed, had been the only candidate with a realistic hope of defeating Richard Nixon in the 1968 Presidential election. Neither Eugene McCarthy, the antiwar candidate, nor Hubert Humphrey, the "Happy

Warrior" from Minnesota, seemed strong enough to successfully challenge the "law and order" campaign being waged by the Republican candidate.

Recognizing that Nixon was likely to become the next President, Warren decided to submit his resignation. He realized that he might not live another four years and concluded that it would be better to cut his service short rather than take the chance of having his old enemy appoint his successor. Warren did not have to consider his income in his decision to resign from the Court. Because he had served more than 10 years on the Court, he would receive a pension equal to his full salary, $40,000 a year. Nor was his health a factor in his decision. Warren was still completely capable of handling all the duties of his office.

On June 13, 1968, the chief justice informed President Johnson of his decision. Officially, he cited age as the reason for his retirement. However, the precise wording of his letter to the President, indicating that his resignation was "effective at your pleasure," suggested to many that his decision was motivated by politics.

This letter from Warren was neither inappropriate nor unusual. Justices often choose to retire or, in many cases, not retire based on who is President and is therefore in a position to select a successor. Depending on the circumstances of their retirement, age or ill health being the most common reasons for leaving the Court, justices may or may not specify the dates for their departure. What made Warren's letter of resignation a lightning rod for criticism was the politically charged atmosphere of the late 1960s and the insistence of conservatives on blaming the social upheaval of the times in large part on the Warren Court.

Political blunders on the part of the President created additional sparks. Johnson's carefully worded response, allowing Warren to stay in office until his successor was approved by the Senate, contributed to the impression that the two men were playing politics. When Johnson nominated Associate Justice Abe Fortas, one of his closest friends and advisors, to succeed Warren and chose Judge Homer Thornberry, the former mayor of Austin, Texas, and another of his political allies, to take Fortas's seat on the Court, Senate conservatives responded with accusations of "double cronyism."

Warren's efforts to explain his own actions and defend the Fortas appointment failed. Fortas made things worse by agreeing to testify before the Senate judiciary committee, a procedure that is now considered a normal part of the nomination process but was at that time still optional. He became a scapegoat, blamed by conservatives for Warren Court decisions, many of them made long before he had joined the Court. During the hearings, Senator Strom Thurmond pointed out that in the 1966-67 term Fortas had voted with Warren in 97 of the 112 decisions made by the Court. "If the Senate confirms this appointment," Thurmond claimed, "we will be confirming an extraconstitutional arrangement by which the Supreme Court justices can so arrange their resignations as to perpetuate their influence and their ideology on the Supreme Court." After four days, the justice declined to answer further questions. The committee eventually voted 11 to 6 to approve the nomination, but the full Senate never had a chance to vote. Faced with a lengthy filibuster, Fortas asked that his nomination be withdrawn.

Stunned by congressional hostility toward his nominee and unwilling to test his political muscle beyond the Fortas fiasco, Johnson asked Warren to remain on the Court "until emotionalism subsides [and] reason and fairness prevail." Warren agreed, but his status remained unclear until after the November elections. As President-elect, Nixon proposed that Warren continue as chief justice until the end of the Supreme Court term, in June 1969. This arrangement, described by the *New York Times* as "sensible and dignified," avoided disrupting the work of the Court and gave Nixon time to choose a successor. It also, according to the *Times,* ended "the confusion about whether the Chief Justice is staying or leaving. . . . By remaining on the bench and then retiring, the Chief Justice helps to remove the Supreme Court from the political category of a captured prize."

On January 20, 1969, Chief Justice Earl Warren had what was for him the dubious honor of administering the Presidential oath of office to Richard M. Nixon. A few months later, Nixon named Warren Burger to take Warren's seat on the Supreme Court. Burger, a Minnesota native with strong conservative credentials, had served on the U.S. Court of Appeals since 1955. At the time of his appointment to the Supreme Court, he was an outspoken critic of the federal judicial system and had published articles calling for reform.

Ironically, Warren's last opinion while serving as chief justice, *Powell* v. *McCormack,* overturned one of Burger's opinions. The House of Representatives, of which John McCormack was the Speaker, had refused to allow Adam Clayton Powell, an African-American minister elected to represent Harlem, to take his seat in Congress. By a vote of 307 to 116, the legislators excluded Powell on the ground that he had misused $40,000 in office funds. Powell filed suit, maintaining that he met the constitutional criteria for serving in the House of Representatives and therefore could not be prevented from representing his district.

*text continues on page 144*

# EARL WARREN RESIGNS

*Earl Warren's decision to resign his seat on the Supreme Court was motivated by political developments in the spring of 1968. At that time President Lyndon B. Johnson decided not to seek a second term in office, and Senator Robert F. Kennedy was assassinated during his quest for the Democratic nomination. Faced with the like-lihood of a Nixon victory in the November election, Warren opted to retire while Johnson could still choose his successor.*

*Critics cited the formal letters exchanged between the chief justice and the President as evidence of a back-room deal. In reality, the reaction resulted in large part from festering wounds caused by the rulings of the Warren Court involving civil rights and liberties.*

*The brief speech Warren delivered at his retirement ceremony acknowledged the controversial nature of many of his opinions but reaffirmed his conviction that a Supreme Court justice should be guided in his work by conscience and the Constitution. Here is an excerpt from Warren's letter of resignation from the Court.*

> When I entered public service 150 million of our 200 million people were not yet born. I, therefore, conceive it my duty to give way to someone who will have more years ahead of him.... I believe there are few people who have enjoyed serving the public or who are more grateful for the opportunity to have done so than I.

*President Johnson replied in this way to Warren's letter of resignation:*

> My dear Chief Justice:
>
> It is with the deepest regret that I learn of your desire to retire, knowing how much the nation has benefited from your service as Chief Justice. However, in deference to your wishes, I will seek a replacement to fill the vacancy in the office of Chief Justice that

will be occasioned when you depart. With your agreement, I will accept your decision to retire effective at such time as a successor is qualified.

*Warren gave the following speech at his retirement ceremony on June 23, 1969:*

I cannot escape the feeling that in one sense, at least, the Court is similar to your [Nixon's] own great office, and that is that so many times it speaks the last word in great governmental affairs.... [I]t is a responsibility that is made more difficult in this Court because we have no constituency. We serve no majority. We serve no minority. We serve only the public interest as we see it, guided only by the Constitution and our own consciences. And conscience is sometimes a very hard taskmaster.

...It is not likely ever, with human nature as it is, for nine men to agree always on the most important and controversial things of life. If it ever comes to such a pass, I would say that the Court will have lost its strength and will no longer be a real force in the affairs of our country. But so long as it is manned by men like those who have preceded us and by others like those who sit today, I have no fear of that ever happening.

Burger acknowledged Congress's power to unseat one of its members. Warren, in contrast, did not hesitate to tackle yet another "political" question. Writing for a 7-to-1 majority, he declared that "the Constitution leaves the House without authority to *exclude* any person duly elected by his constituents, who meets all the requirements for membership expressly prescribed by the Constitution." The decision, announced on June 16, 1969, not only upheld the rules essential to the democratic process but also affirmed yet again the Court's power to intervene when the other branches of government overstep their constitutional authority.

On June 23, President Nixon attended the final session of the Warren Court. Standing at the lectern provided for lawyers, dressed in striped trousers and a cutaway jacket, he spoke of Warren's dignity, fairness, integrity, and humanity. Following brief remarks regarding the Court and its role in the U.S. government, Warren administered the oath of office to his successor. When asked later that day how he would like the Warren Court to be remembered, the former chief responded, "As the People's Court."

A few days later, a national tribute to Warren was held on the steps of the Lincoln Memorial. In addition to entertainment provided by the U.S. Army Chorus, friends and colleagues spoke of Warren's contributions. Eric Sevareid, a well-known essayist and television news commentator, praised Warren for possessing "that certain quality that helps to hold a diverse people together and move a nation on." Warren, he explained, had what the Romans called *gravitas:* "patience, stability, weight of judgment, breadth of shoulders[,]. . . that strength of the few that makes life possible for many[,]. . . manhood."

Following his retirement, Earl and Nina Warren remained in Washington, D.C. The justice moved into a smaller office at the Supreme Court and hired only one clerk each year, who served primarily as a speechwriter. Over the next few years Warren traveled extensively, both in the United States and overseas. He received numerous awards, attended a variety of conferences, and spoke frequently to college under-graduates and law students.

Warren's interest in international relations, first aroused during the opening meetings of the United Nations held in San Francisco in 1945, had developed during his time on the Court. Beginning in 1953, he and Nina had spent their summers traveling to other countries, usually to attend inter-national judicial conferences.

In retirement, he continued to play an active role in the organization called World Peace Through Law that he had helped found in 1963. This organization, now a part of the World Jurist Association, is concerned with a wide range of legal issues, including ratification and implementation of arms control agreements and human rights treaties, the use of compulsory arbitration to resolve disputes between nations, adoption and enforcement of international criminal codes, enactment of laws governing narcotics and dangerous drugs, and freedom for lawyers throughout the world to carry out their professional duties without government interference. Warren attended every one of the biennial meetings held in cities around the world, including Abidjan, Ivory Coast; Bangkok, Thailand; and Belgrade, Yugoslavia. In 1973 the organization gave him its first Human Rights Award. He also served as the first president of the World Association of Judges, an organization of judges and lawyers from 117 countries affiliated with World Peace Through Law and dedicated to establishing the legal basis for world peace.

Despite this interest in world peace, domestic affairs dom-inated Warren's thinking in his last years. Two issues in par-ticular demanded his attention. The first was a proposal for a National Court of Appeals. Chief Justice Burger appointed a committee in 1971 to review the work of the Supreme Court and recommend reforms. Under a proposal made by the committee, judges from the federal Courts of Appeal—rather than Supreme Court justices, assisted by their law

*Warren spoke at the dedication of Storke Tower at the University of California, Santa Barbara, in 1969. The Warren family had close ties to the University of California. Virginia, like her father, graduated from Berkeley. Earl Jr. and Bobby attended Davis; Dorothy and Honey Bear went to UCLA.*

clerks—would decide which cases the high court would hear. Warren, who labeled the proposal "naïve" and "dangerous," campaigned actively for its defeat. According to Justice Brennan, the former chief was convinced that the National Court of Appeals "threatened to shut the door of the Supreme Court on the poor, the friendless, the little man."

The second domestic issue to involve Warren was the Watergate break-in. During the 1972 Presidential campaign, burglars were discovered breaking in to the Democratic campaign headquarters in Washington, D.C., which were located in the Watergate apartment building and office complex. The burglars turned out to have CIA and White House connections, facts that inevitably raised questions about President Nixon's involvement. Although Nixon's actual role was never determined, the efforts to cover up who was responsible for the break-in led to investigations by the FBI, the Department of Justice, Congress, and the courts. In an effort to squelch rumors and silence criticism, President Nixon appointed Archibald Cox to serve as special prosecutor. However, Nixon's refusal to turn over tape recordings of official conversations led Cox, along with the attorney general and his deputy, to resign. Cox's successor, Leon Jaworski, turned to the courts for a ruling on whether Nixon should be compelled to release the recordings.

As the saga of Watergate unfolded before the public, Warren became increasingly concerned by the impact it was having on the nation. In the winter and spring of 1974, Warren traveled to college campuses around the country. Despite declining health—he had begun to develop heart problems—he was reluctant to cancel appearances but took occasional breaks when he needed time to recuperate from his grueling schedule. Warren was convinced that the growing distrust of government caused by the Watergate investigation was of such magnitude that it could not be ignored. He visited Stanford University and the University of Santa Clara in California to talk to students about the scandal. He was, however, forced to cancel an appearance at an NAACP dinner to commemorate the 20th anniversary of the *Brown* v. *Board of Education* decision.

At the end of May 1974, Warren gave the commencement address at Morehouse College in Atlanta. Repeating the message he had been spreading for months, he reminded the graduates that "a humble night watchman who was not susceptible to bribery" was responsible for the investigations of wrongdoing in the Watergate matter, and urged them to employ democratic means to correct the problems that were plaguing government. "The great virtue of our government," he asserted, "is that people...elect our representatives on all levels of government....When they have made a mistake, they can rectify it." This was his last public appearance.

Confined first to his home and then later to a hospital in the capital, Warren remained preoccupied with events relating to Watergate. The most pressing question was whether the Supreme Court would grant Nixon's claim of "executive privilege" and allow him to withhold the tape recordings of White House conversations. The judiciary,

Warren contended, was the final arbiter of the law and the President was not above the law. "No man, not even a king," the former chief told his friend Arthur Goldberg, "can put himself above the law. I am confident the Court will do its duty—and so will the nation."

The following day, July 9, justices Brennan and Douglas visited Warren in the hospital. They had just left a conference where the justices had voted 8 to 0 (William Rehnquist did not participate in the decision) to compel Nixon to turn over the tapes. After sharing the news, they departed, knowing that Warren fully supported the action the Court had taken. Later that evening, Warren died.

Nine thousand people filed by the bronze, flag-draped casket that was placed in the Great Hall of the Supreme Court later that week. A thousand attended the funeral service held at the National Cathedral. Among his mourners were Supreme Court justices, former law clerks, family, friends, and his lifelong foe Richard Nixon. Clergy from the Episcopal, Jewish, and Roman Catholic faiths honored the former chief justice of the United States, a man who seldom attended church but who kept a copy of the Bible next to his reading chair and lived a life consistent with its teachings. Following the service, Warren was buried with full military honors in Arlington National Cemetery.

On July 24, Chief Justice Burger opened a special session of the Supreme Court with a short speech honoring Earl Warren. The next item of business, an announcement of the Court's ruling in *United States* v. *Nixon,* signaled the Court's continued commitment to "equal justice under law."

# CHRONOLOGY

**March 19, 1891**
Born in Los Angeles, California

**1896**
Moves with family to Bakersfield, California

**August 1908**
Enters the University of California, Berkeley

**April 1917**
Inducted into the U.S. Army

**May 1, 1920**
Begins working in the office of the district attorney for
Alameda County, California

**October 14, 1925**
Marries Nina Palmquist Meyers

**January 1939**
Becomes attorney general of California

**January 1943**
Is inaugurated as governor of California

**1948**
Republicans nominate him as candidate for Vice President

**1952**
Campaigns unsucessfully for the Republican Presidential
nomination

**September 27, 1953**
Is appointed chief justice of the United States

**May 17, 1954**
Supreme Court decides *Brown* v. *Board of Education of
Topeka, Kansas*

**June 17, 1957**
"Red Monday"—Supreme Court decides *Watkins* v. *United
States, Sweezy* v. *New Hampshire, Yates* v. *United States,* and
*Service* v. *Dulles*

**June 24, 1957**
Supreme Court decides *Roth* v. *United States* and *Kingsley Books*
v. *Brown*

**March 26, 1962**
Supreme Court decides *Baker* v. *Carr*

**March 18, 1963**
Supreme Court decides *Gideon* v. *Wainwright*

**November 22, 1963**
President John F. Kennedy is assassinated

**November 29, 1963**
President Lyndon B. Johnson establishes the U.S. Commission to Report upon the Assassination of President John F. Kennedy; Warren is appointed chair of the commission

**June 15, 1964**
Supreme Court decides *Reynolds* v. *Sims*

**June 22, 1964**
Supreme Court decides *Escobedo* v. *Illinois*

**June 13, 1966**
Supreme Court decides *Miranda* v. *Arizona*

**June 16, 1969**
Supreme Court decides *Powell* v. *McCormack*

**June 23, 1969**
Warren retires from Supreme Court

**July 9, 1974**
Dies in Washington, D.C.

# FURTHER READING

## WORKS WRITTEN BY EARL WARREN

Christman, Henry M., ed. *The Public Papers of Chief Justice Earl Warren*. New York: Capricorn, 1966.

Warren, Earl. *Memoirs*. Garden City, N.Y.: Doubleday, 1977.

## BIOGRAPHIES OF EARL WARREN

Cray, Ed. *Chief Justice: A Biography of Earl Warren*. New York: Simon & Schuster, 1997.

Katcher, Leo. *Earl Warren: A Political Biography*. New York: McGraw-Hill, 1967.

Pollock, Jack Harrison. *Earl Warren: The Judge Who Changed America*. Englewood Cliffs, N.J.: Prentice-Hall, 1979.

White, G. Edward. *Earl Warren: A Public Life*. New York: Oxford University Press, 1982.

## WORKS ABOUT THE WARREN COURT

Bickel, Alexander M. *Politics and the Warren Court*. New York: Harper & Row, 1965.

Cox, Archibald. *The Warren Court: Constitutional Decision as an Instrument of Reform*. Cambridge: Harvard University Press, 1968.

Goldberg, Arthur. *Equal Justice: The Warren Era of the Supreme Court*. New York: Farrar, Straus & Giroux, 1971.

Horwitz, Morton. *The Warren Court and the Pursuit of Justice*. New York: Hill & Wang, 1998.

Powe, Lucas A., Jr. *The Warren Court and American Politics*. Cambridge: Belknap Press of Harvard University Press, 2000.

Schwartz, Bernard. *Superchief: Earl Warren and His Supreme Court—A Judicial Biography*. New York: New York University Press, 1983.

Schwartz, Bernard, and Stephen Lesher. *Inside the Supreme Court*. Garden City, N.Y.: Doubleday, 1983.

## Related Reading

Ashmore, Harry S. *Hearts and Minds: A Personal Chronicle of Race in America*. Cabin John, Md.: Seven Locks Press, 1988.

Baker, Liva. *Miranda: Crime, Law, and Politics*. New York: Atheneum, 1983.

Irons, Peter. *Justice at War: The Story of the Japanese American Internment Cases*. Berkeley: University of California Press, 1983.

Kluger, Richard. *Simple Justice: The History of* Brown v. Board of Education *and Black America's Struggle for Equality*. New York: Vintage, 1975.

Morgan, Donald. *Congress and the Constitution*. Cambridge: Harvard University Press, 1966.

Mowry, George. *The California Progressives*. Berkeley: University of California Press, 1951.

Murphy, Paul L. *The Constitution in Crisis Times, 1918–1969*. New York: Harper & Row, 1972.

Patterson, James T. Brown v. Board of Education: *A Civil Rights Milestone and Its Troubled Legacy*. New York: Oxford University Press, 2001.

Rehnquist, William T. "When the Laws Were Silent." *American Heritage,* October 1998, 76–89.

———. *All the Laws by One: Civil Liberties in Wartime*. New York: Vintage, 1998.

Sabin, Arthur J. *In Calmer Times: The Supreme Court and Red Monday*. Philadelphia: University of Pennsylvania Press, 1999.

Urofsky, Melvin I. *The Continuity of Change*. Belmont, Calif.: Wadsworth, 1991.

Wilkinson, J. Harvie. *Serving Justice*. New York: Charterhouse, 1974.

# INDEX

# ACKNOWLEDGMENTS

I was first introduced to Chief Justice Warren, in a formal way, by Professor Donald G. Morgan. As a political science major at Mount Holyoke College during Warren's last years on the Court, I became acquainted with the chief justice in Mr. Morgan's courses on American political thought, constitutional law, and church–state issues. I was greatly impressed by his remarkable understanding of the cases we studied and the issues we explored, but, even more, I appreciated his efforts to help students understand the implications of the Court's decisions. Like the chief justice whom he so admired, Mr. Morgan realized the importance of studying not only the technical aspects of the law but also the impact of judicial rulings on real people. His classes taught me the practical value of the humanities, and these lessons continue to shape my scholarly work.

I did most of the research for this book in Wilson Library at Western Washington University, with the assistance of a team of reference librarians who guided me to helpful resources and took a genuine interest in the work that was underway. The service provided by the staff in the Manuscript Division of the Library of Congress also made my detective work enjoyable and rewarding.

Above all, I am grateful for the love and encouragement of my husband, Stephen V. Senge. His confidence in my ability, joy in my progress, and patience with my challenges made all the difference!

# PICTURE CREDITS

AP/Wide World: 74, 110; Arizona State Library, Archives and Public Records, Archives Division, Phoenix: 120 (#R1-3J68); Courtesy of the Bancroft Library, University of California, Berkeley: 8, 11, 18, 45, 51; California State Archives: 42, 52; Dwight D. Eisenhower Library: 157; Fort Lewis Military Museum: 16; Courtesy of Special Collections Department, Harvard Law School Library: 81 Kansas State Historical Society: 66; John F. Kennedy Library: 102; Courtesy of Kern County Museum, Used by Permission: 12; Library of Congress: 20, 62, 78, 82, 106, 116; National Japanese American Historical Society: 39; Copyright The New Yorker Collection 1964 Lee Lorenz from cartoonbank.com: 122; Pasadena Tournament of Roses: 97; Supreme Court Archives: 2, 22, 30, 124, 131; Tennessee State Library and Archives: 112; Timepix: 69 (Carl Iwasaki), 95 (Bob Gomel), 105 (Art Rickerby); University Archives, University of California, Santa Barbara: 138; University of New Hampshire Library: 89.

# TEXT CREDITS

Lessons from History: The San Francisco Graft Prosecution, p. 28: *Earl Warren, Memoirs,* p. 91.

Warren on Lincoln, pp. 60–61: Earl Warren, "Lincoln Day Address," in Henry M. Christman, ed., *The Public Papers of Chief Justice Earl Warren,* 1966, pp. 31–39.

McCarthyism and the Threat to Free Speech, p. 91: *The Public Papers of Chief Justice Earl Warren,* pp. 55–61

An Executive Apology, pp. 99–100: Earl Warren, 104 Manuscript Division, Library of Congress.

Public Recognition, p. 113: Earl Warren, 104 Manuscript Division, Library of Congress.

The *Miranda* Principles, p. 136 Earl Warren, Manuscript Division, Library of Congress.

Earl Warren Resigns, p. 142: Jack Harrison Pollock, *Earl Warren: The Judge Who Changed America,* 1979, pp. 275–76, 278, 294; Ed Cray, *Chief Justice: A Biography of Earl Warren,* 1997, p. 513.

**Christine L. Compston** is on the faculty of the department of history at the University of Massachusetts—Boston. Compston began her teaching career at Gould Academy and Phillips Exeter. She has since taught at Clark University, the University of New Hampshire, and Western Washington University, and has been a Fulbright Scholar in Norway. More recently, she served as Director of the National History Education Network and as a consultant for the PBS quiz show *Where in Time Is Carmen Sandiego?* She is the co-editor of *Holmes and Frankfurter: Their Correspondence, 1912–1934.*